COLORING BOOK

THIS COLORING BOOK BELONGS TO :

....

....

COLOR ME !

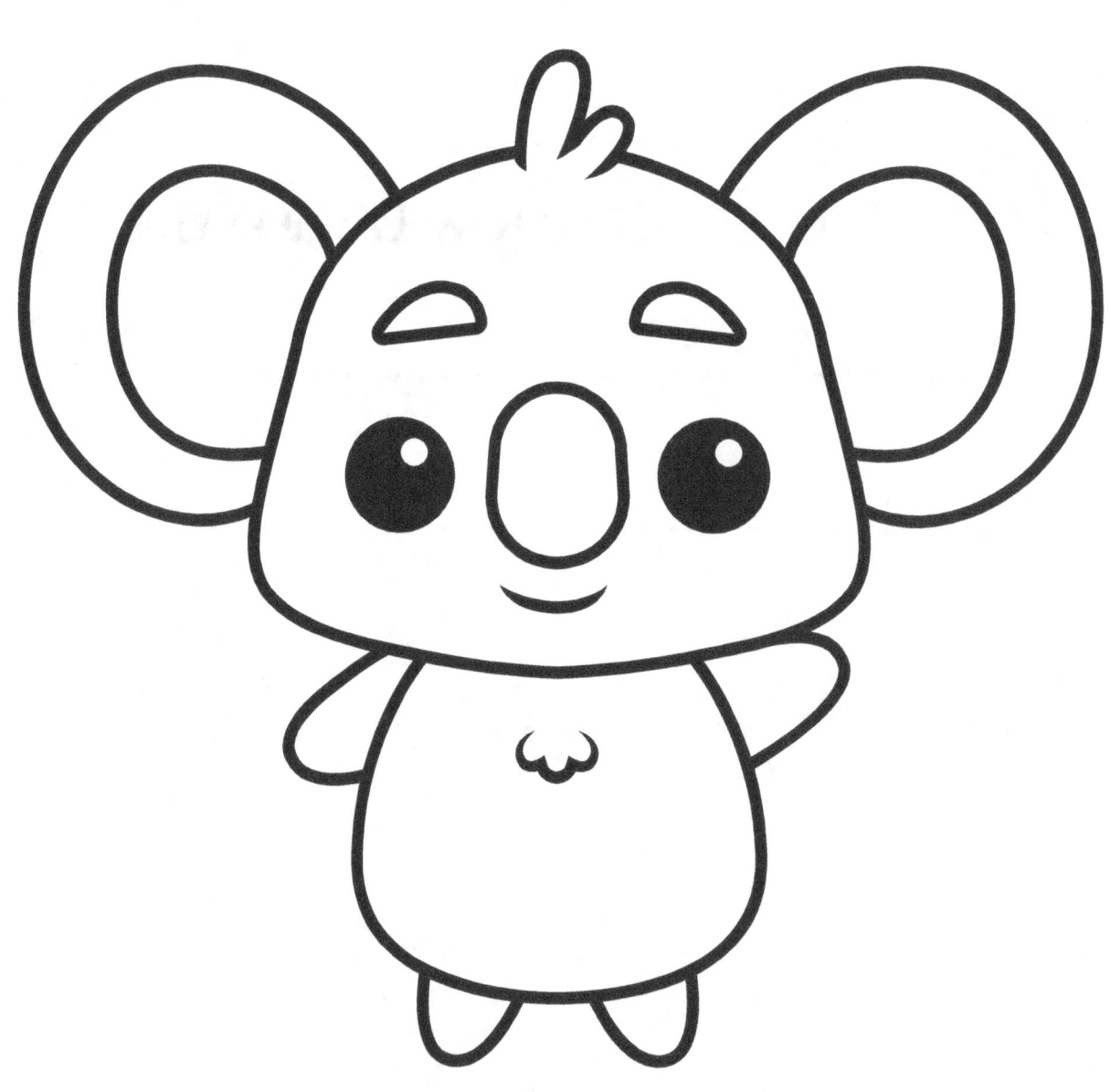

COLOR ME !

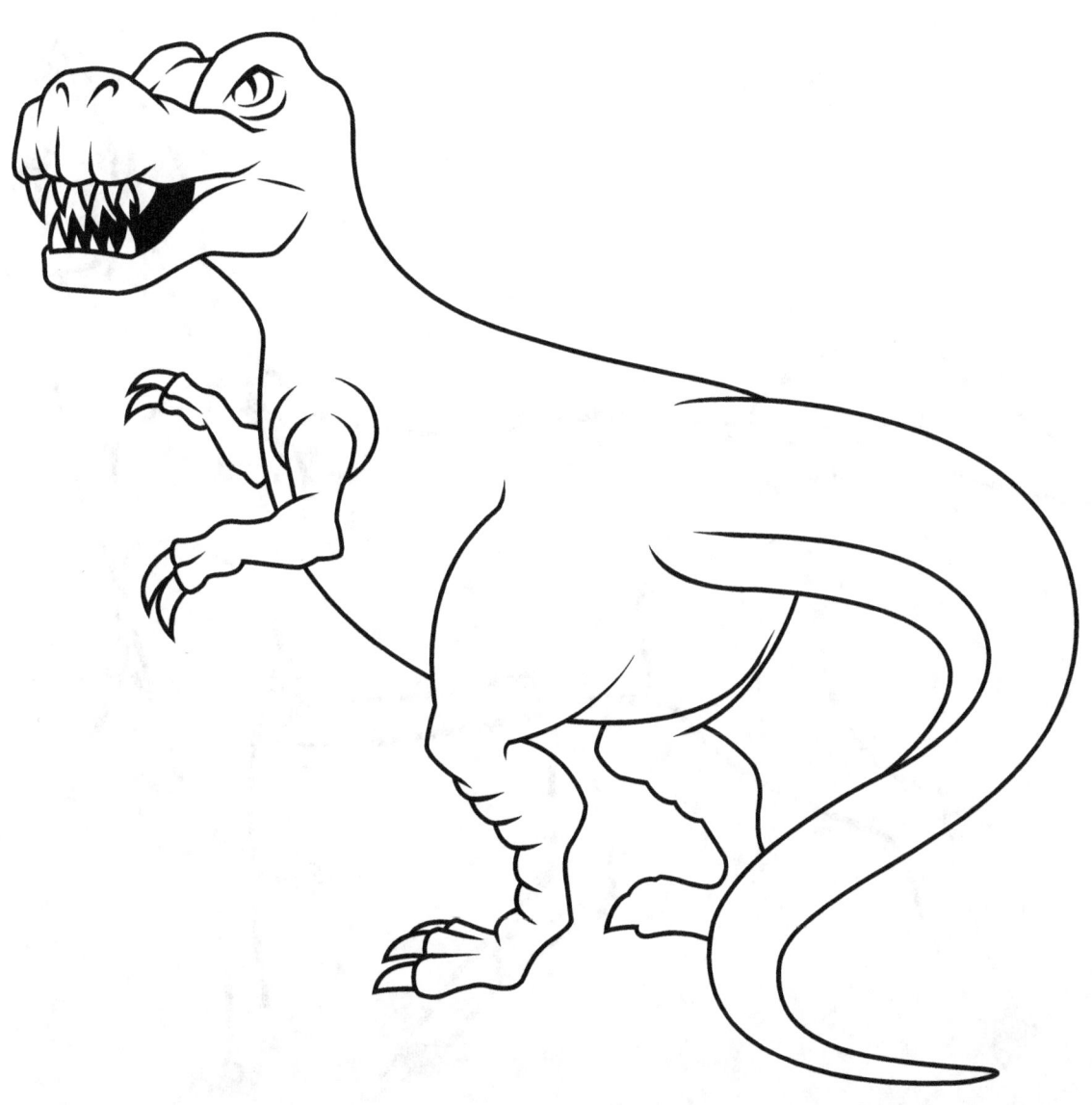

COLOR ME !

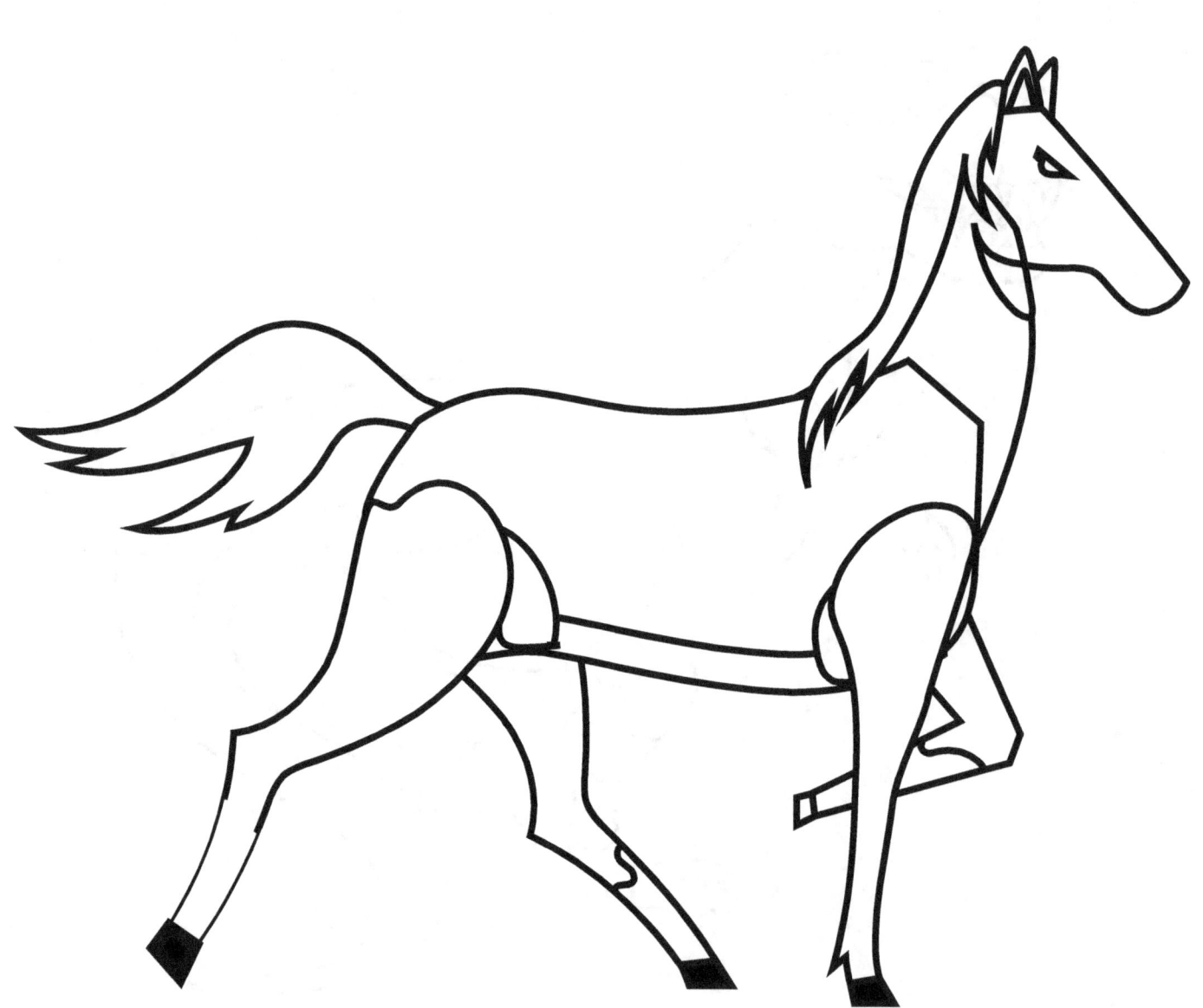

COLOR ME !

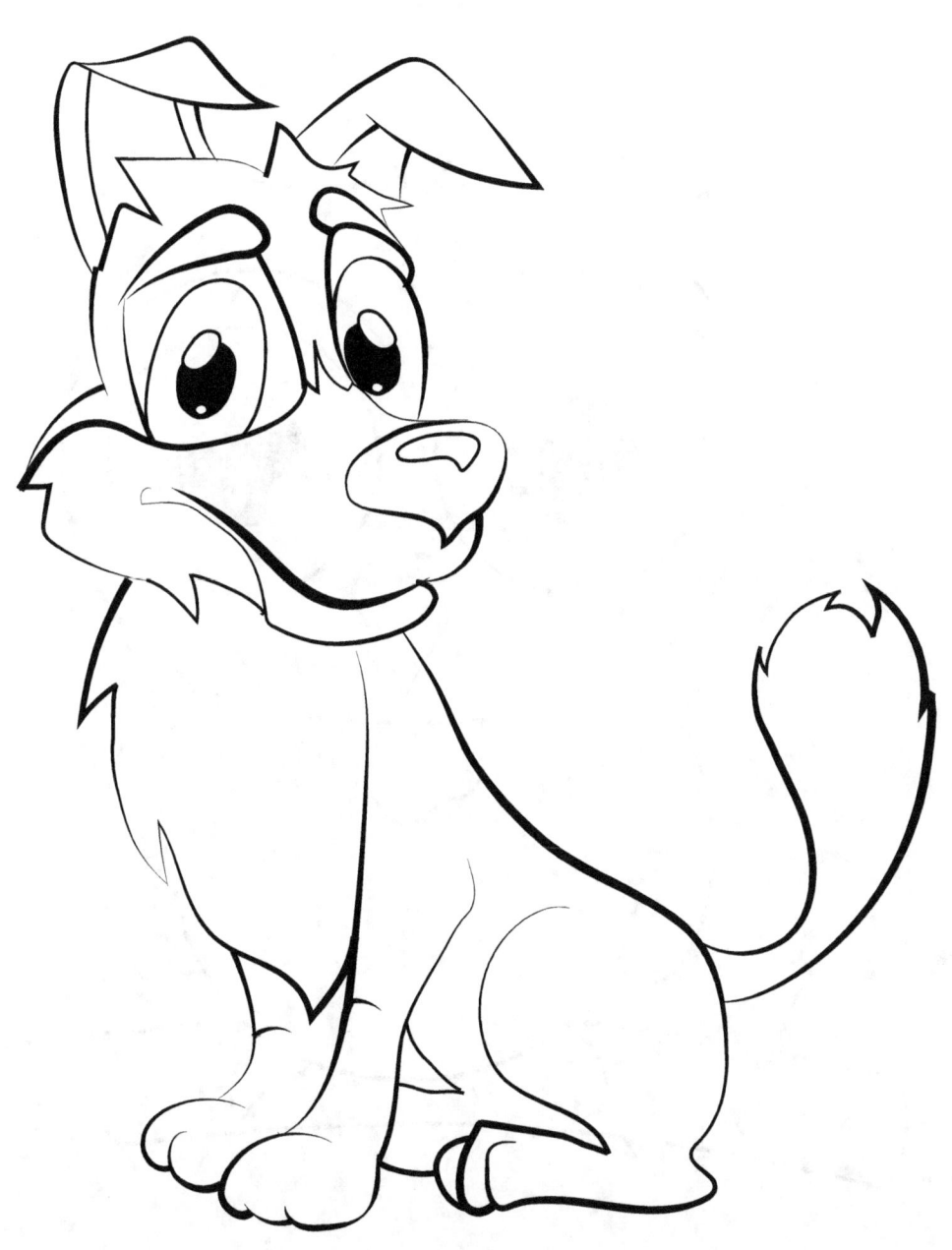

COLOR ME !

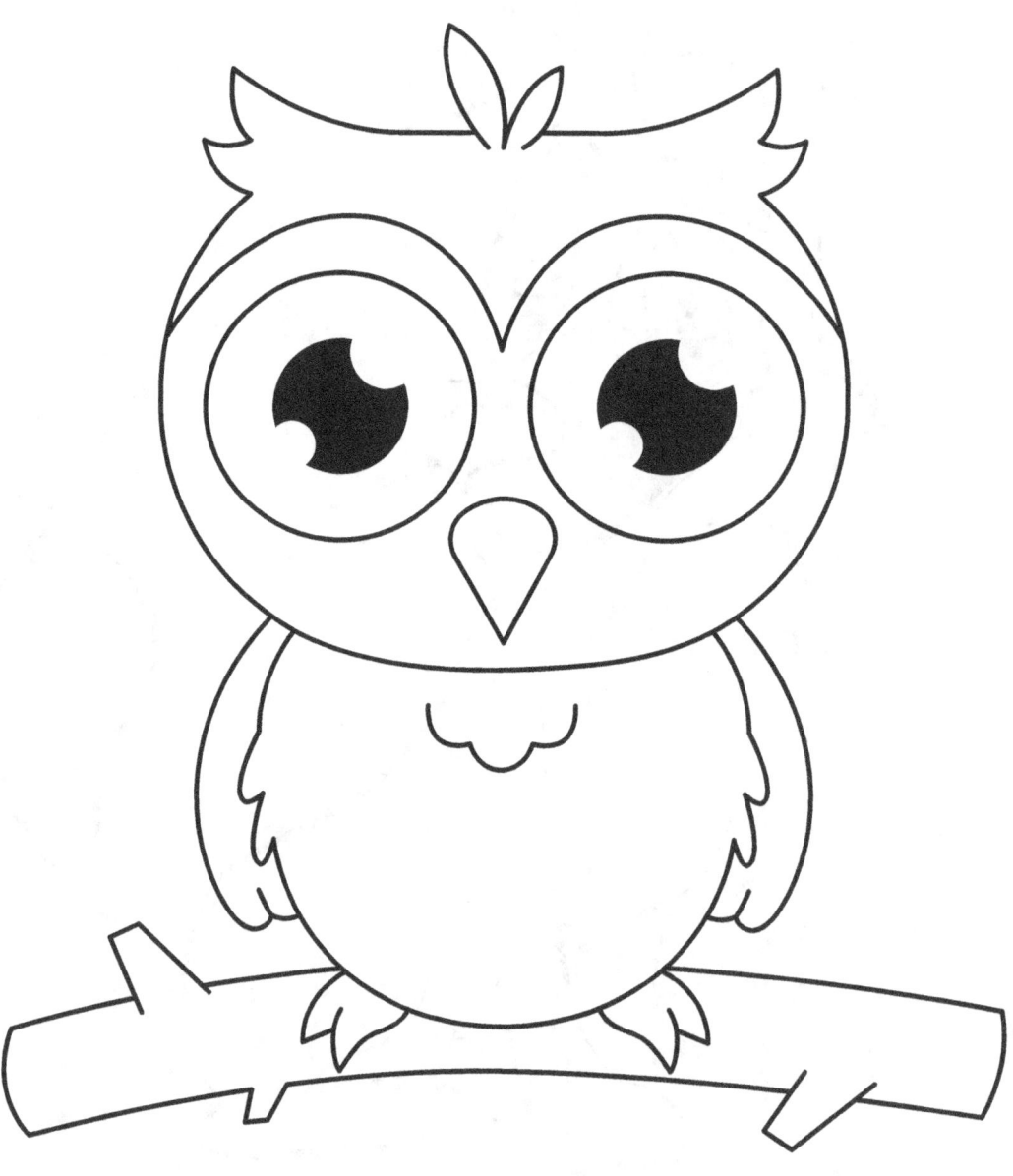

COLOR ME !

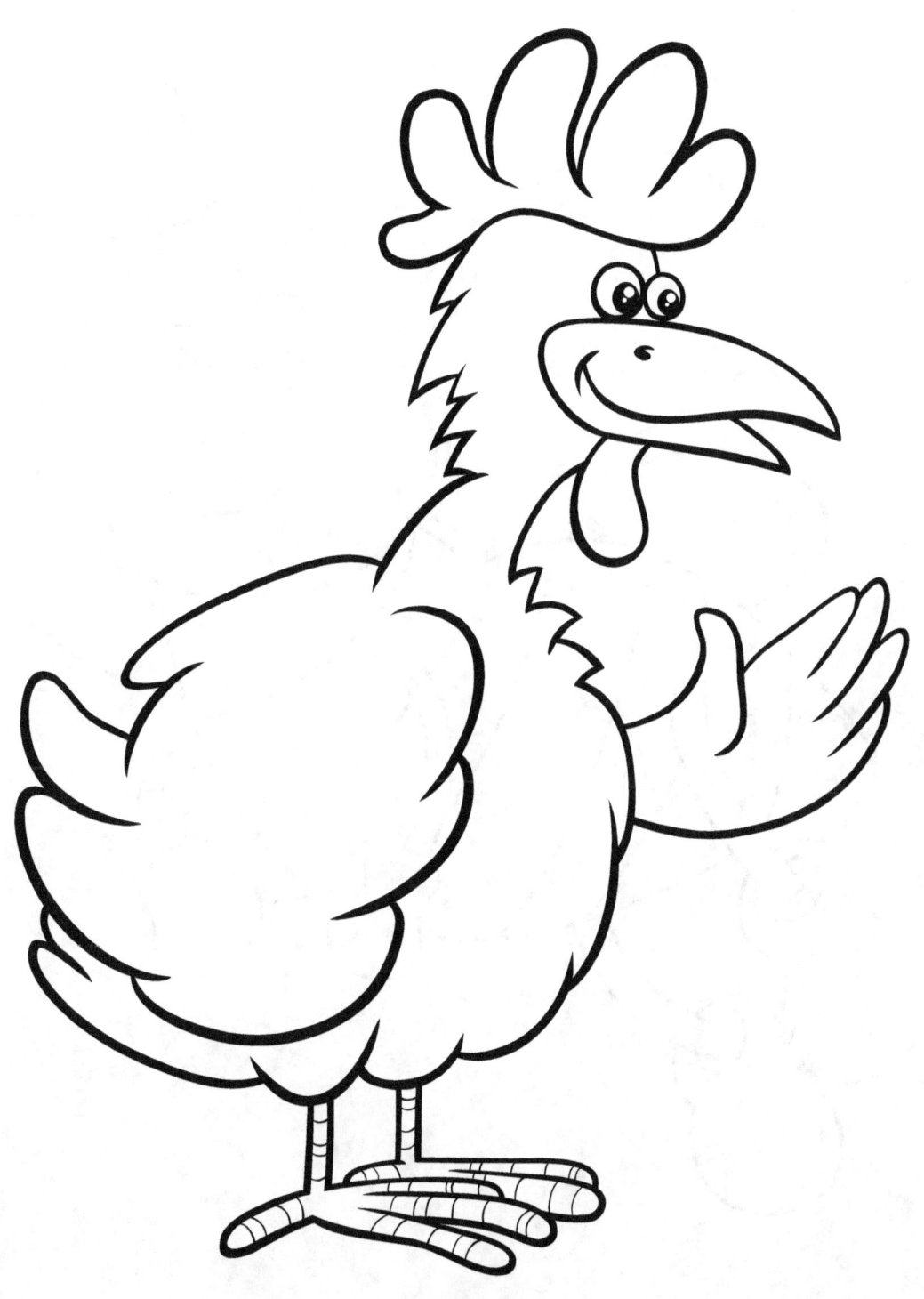

COLOR ME !

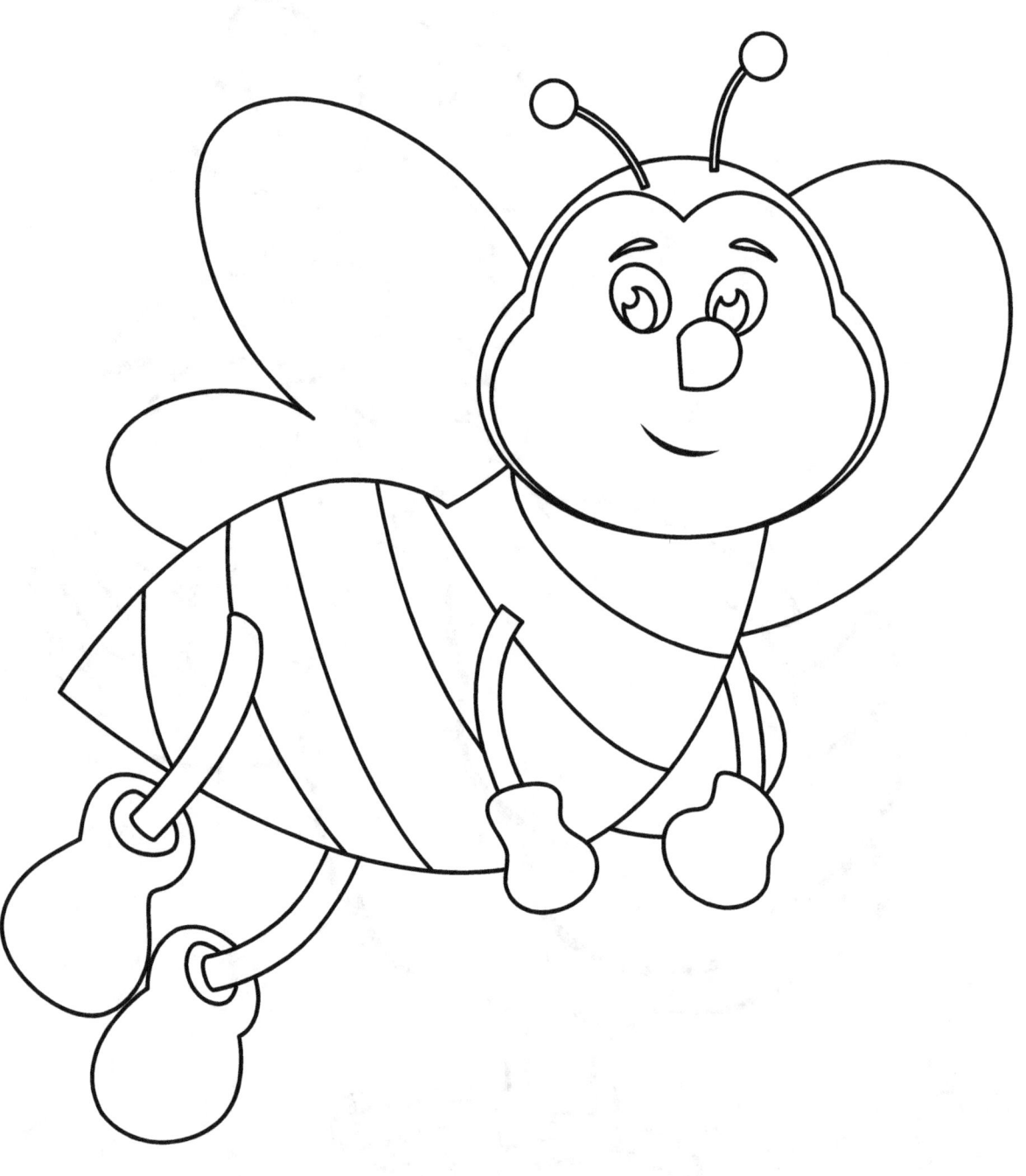

COLOR ME !

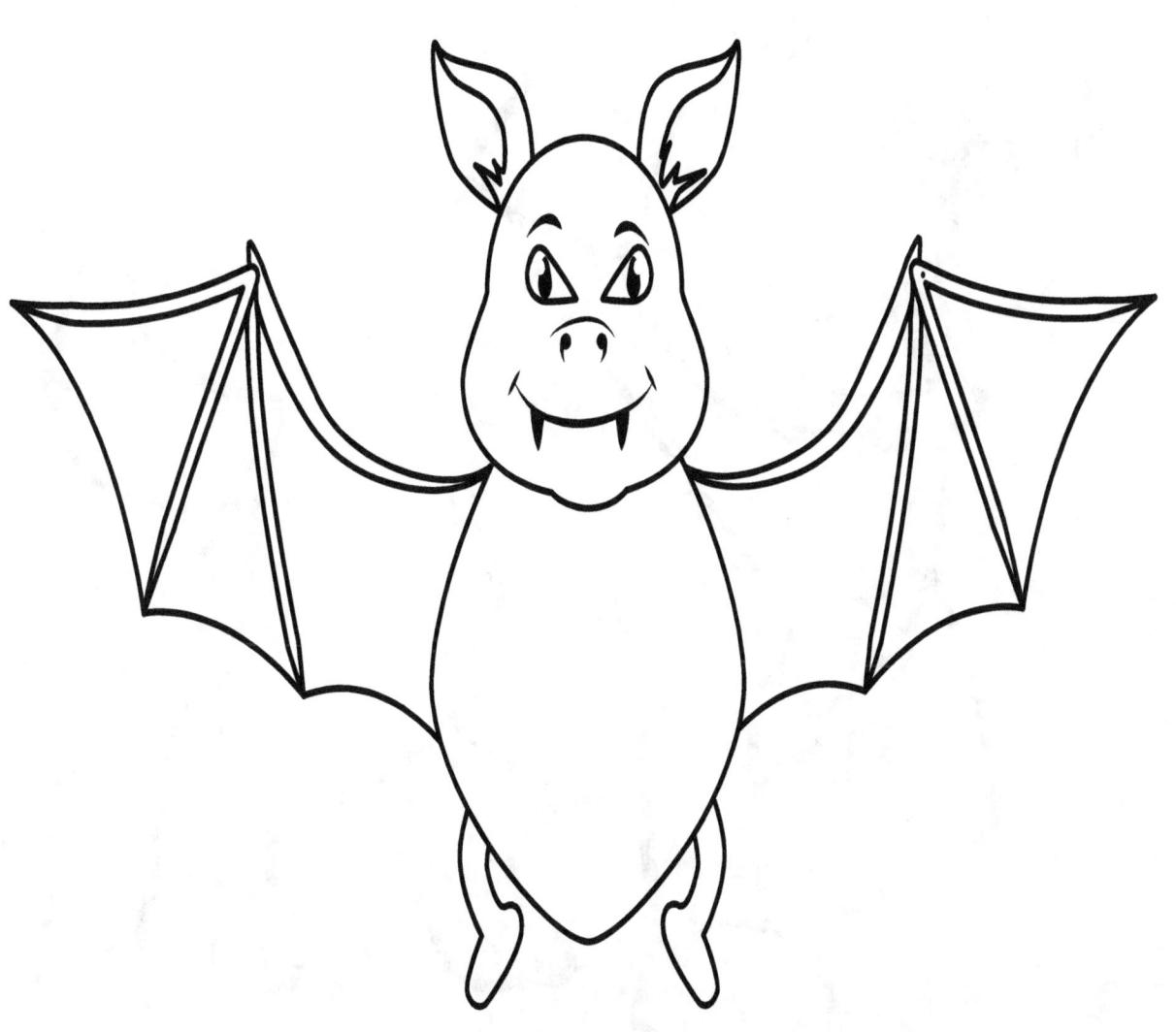

COLOR ME !

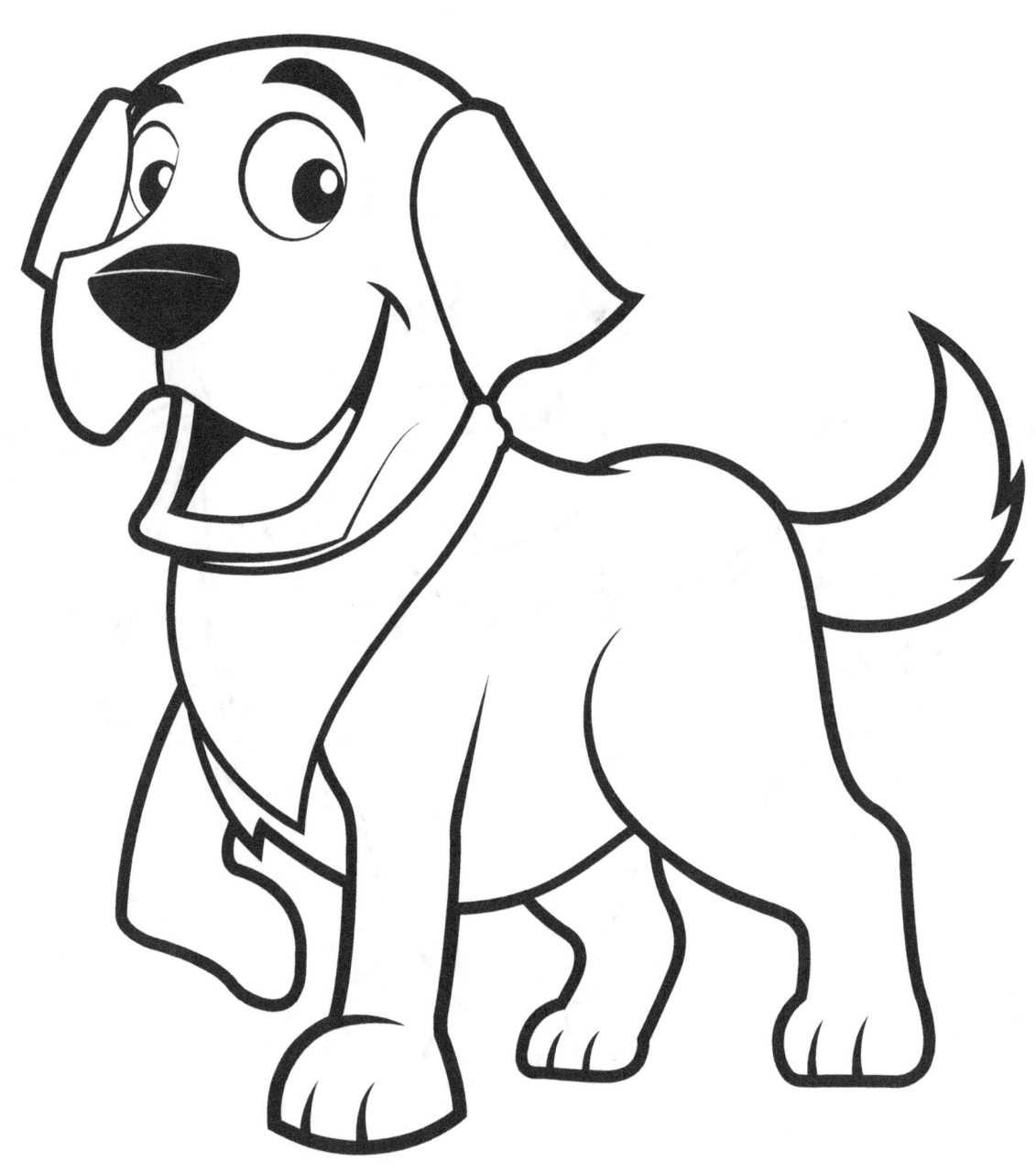

COLOR ME !

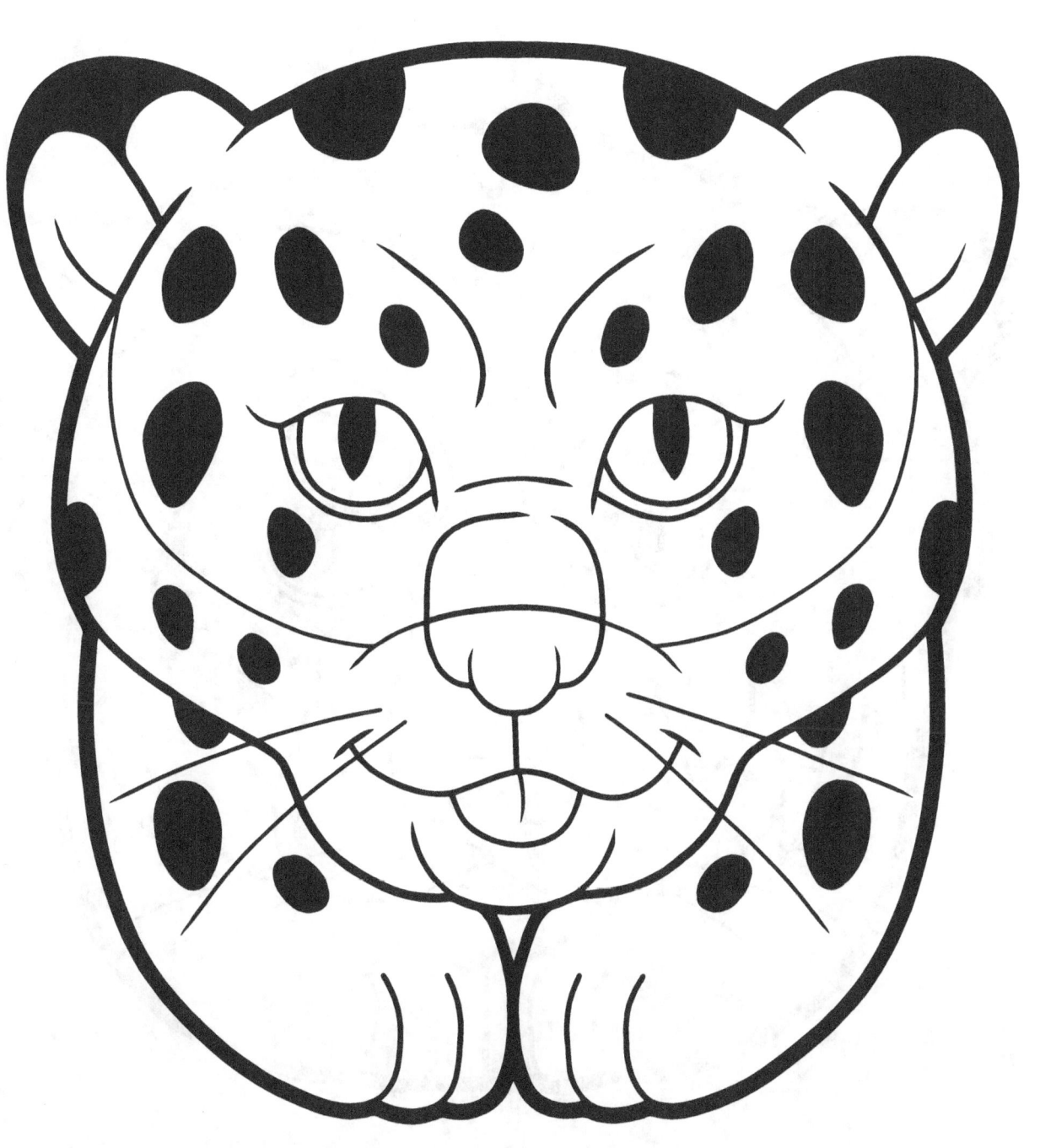

COLOR ME !

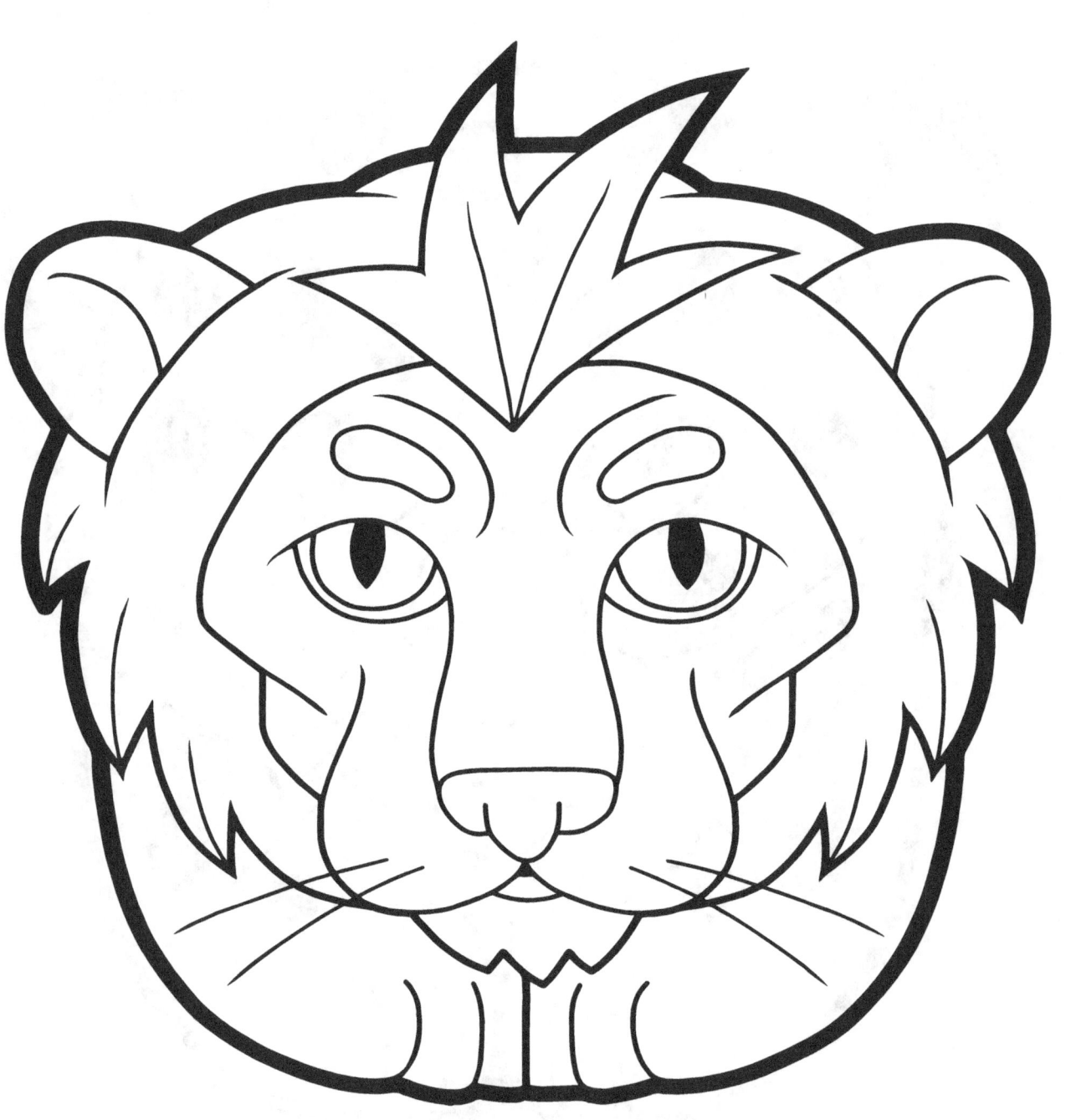

COLOR ME !

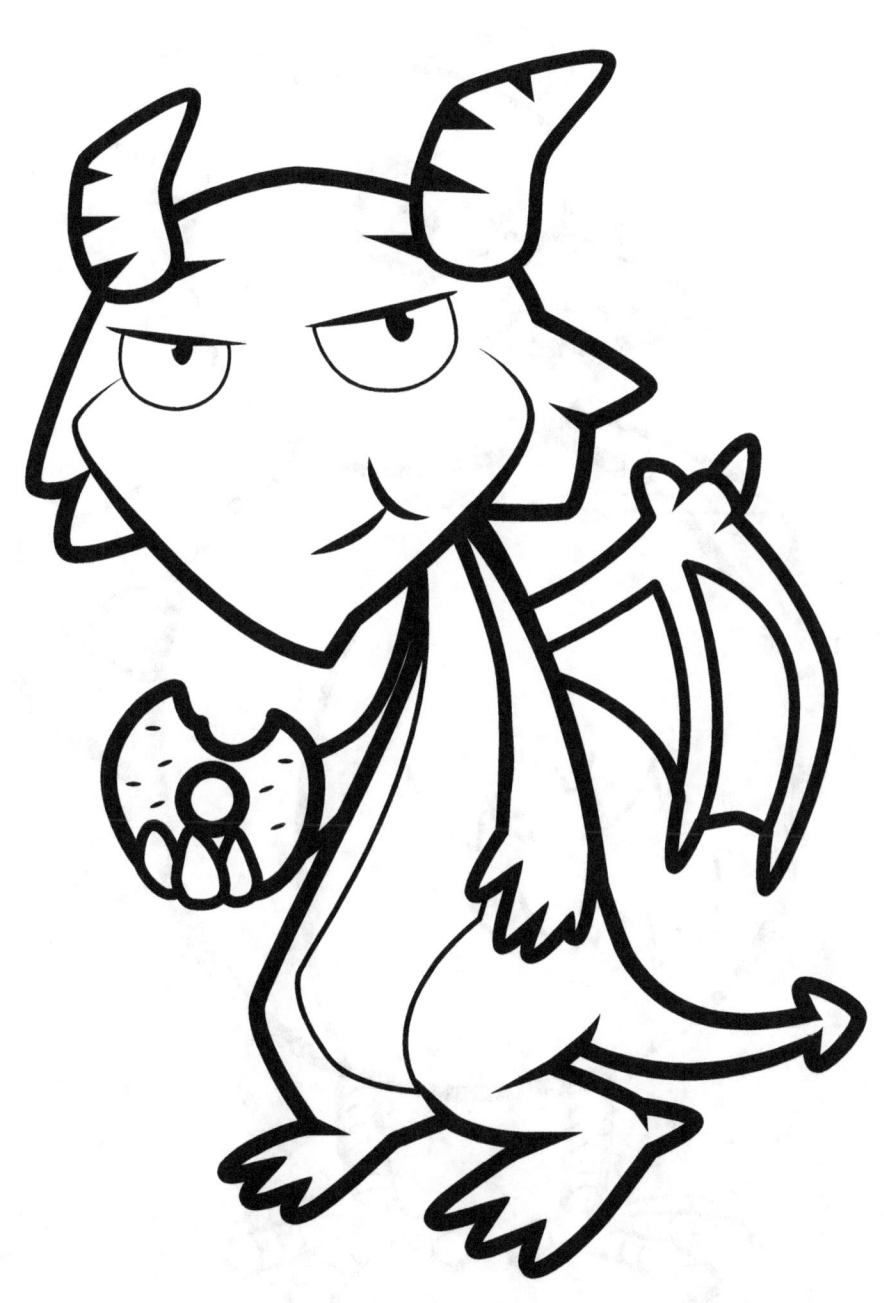

COLOR ME !

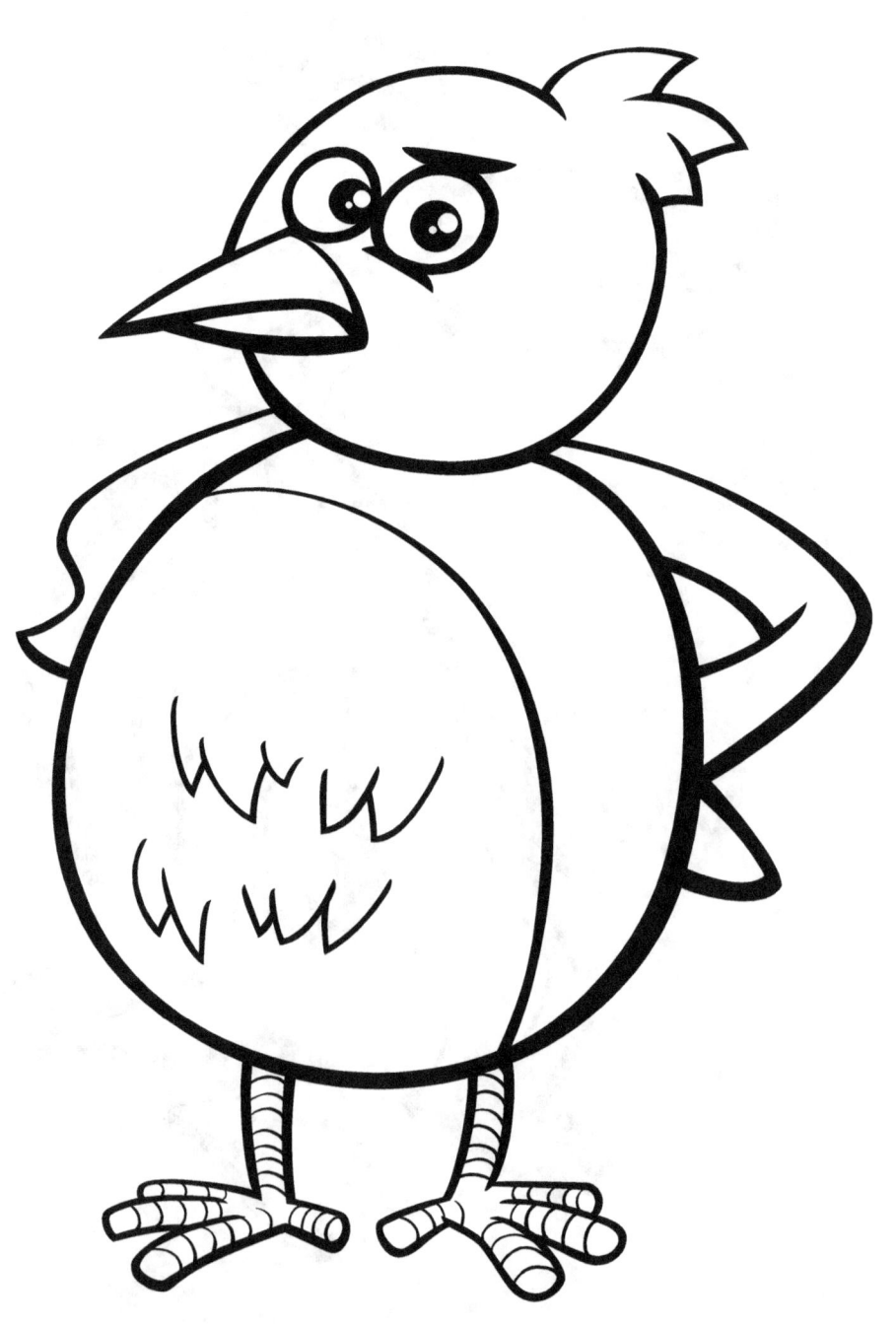

COLOR ME !

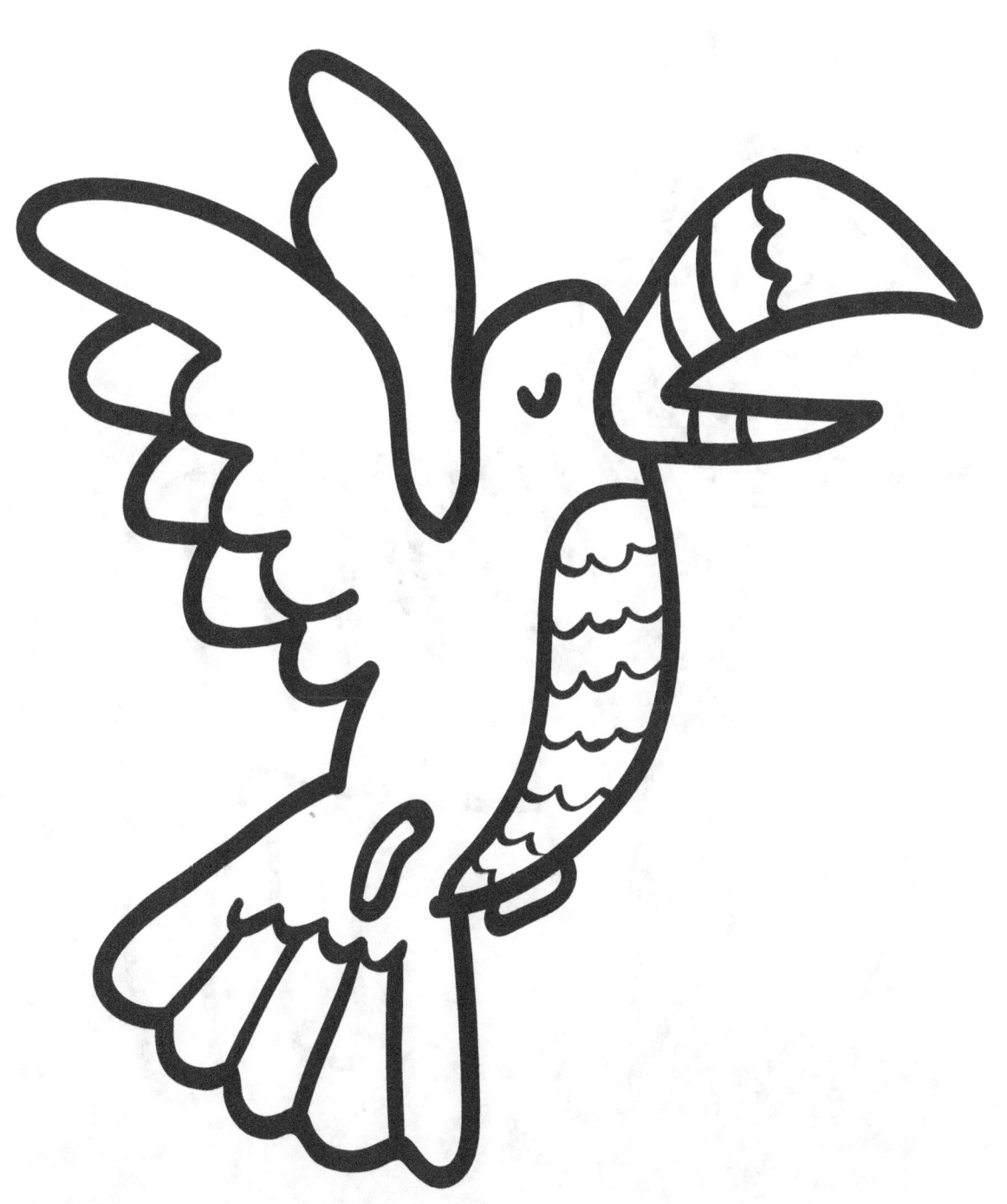

COLOR ME !

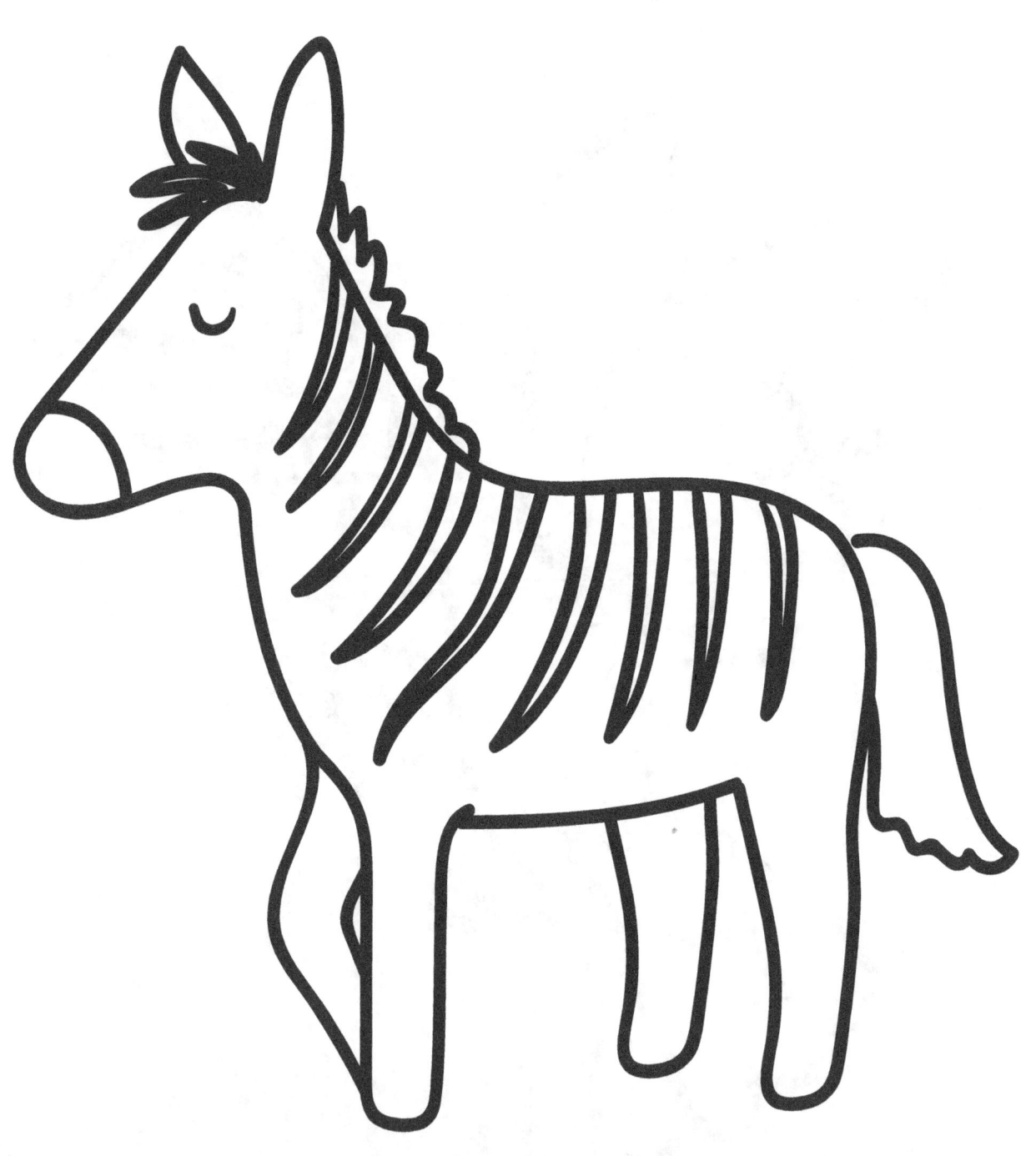

COLOR ME !

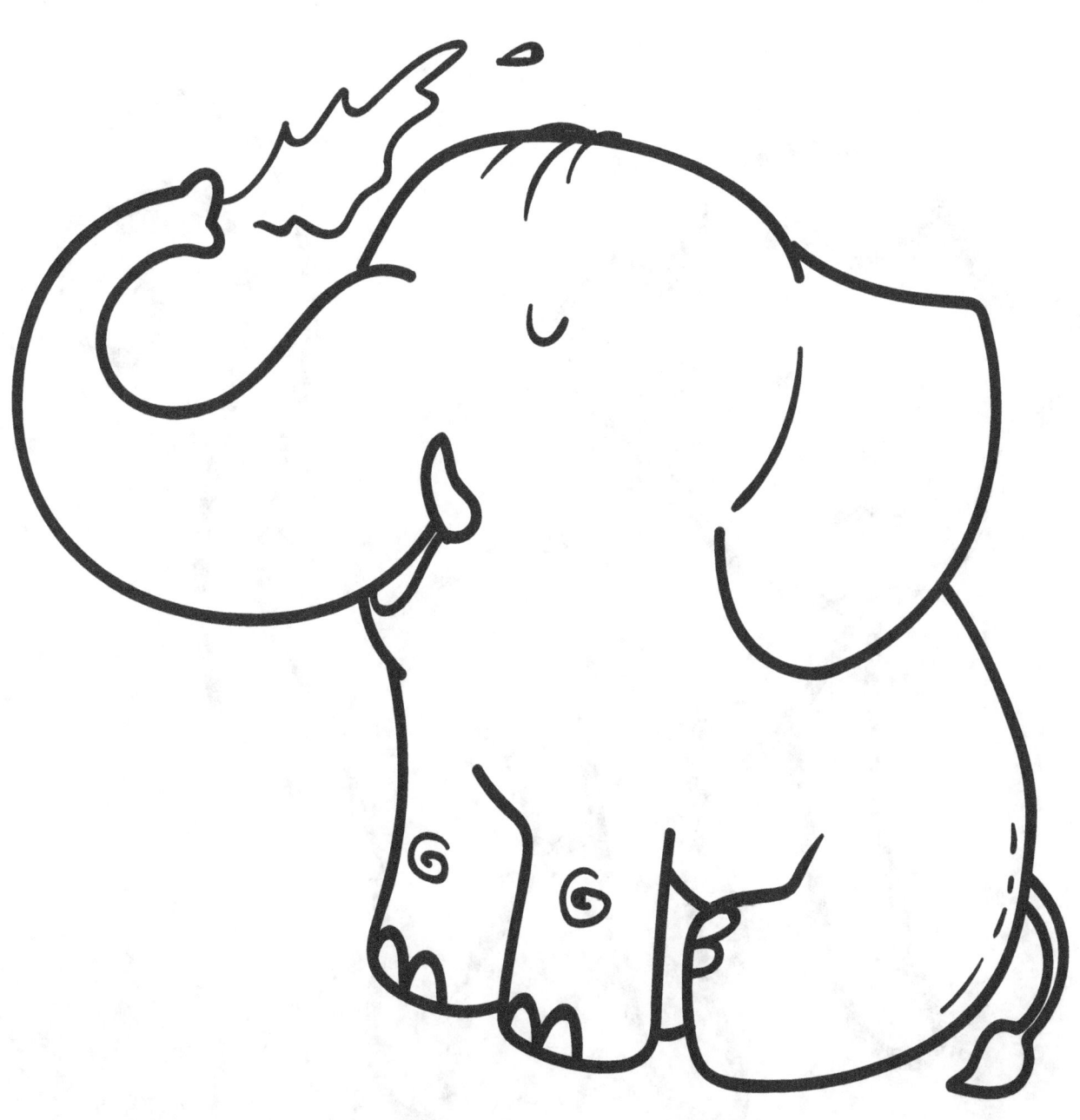

COLOR ME !

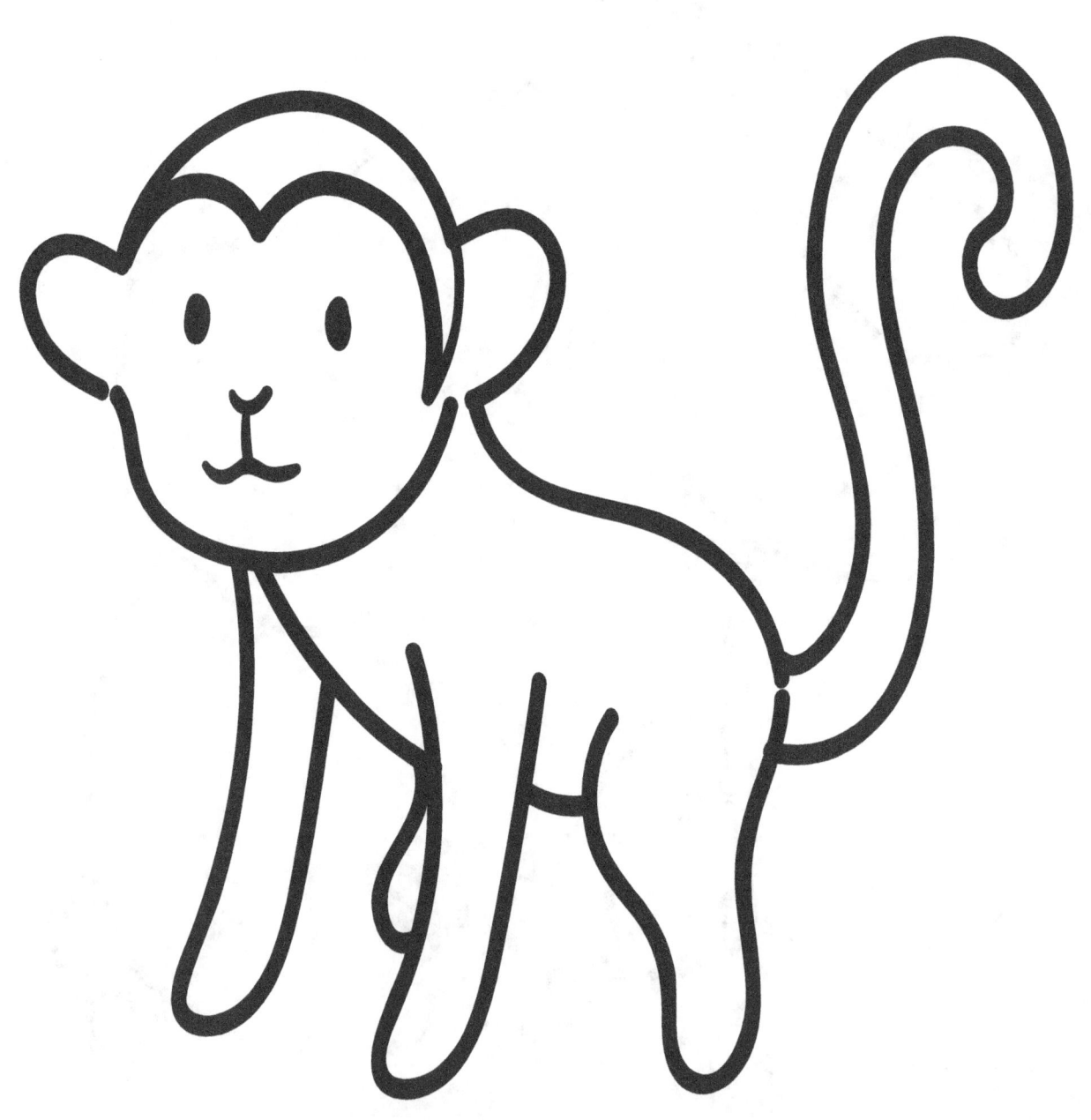

COLOR ME !

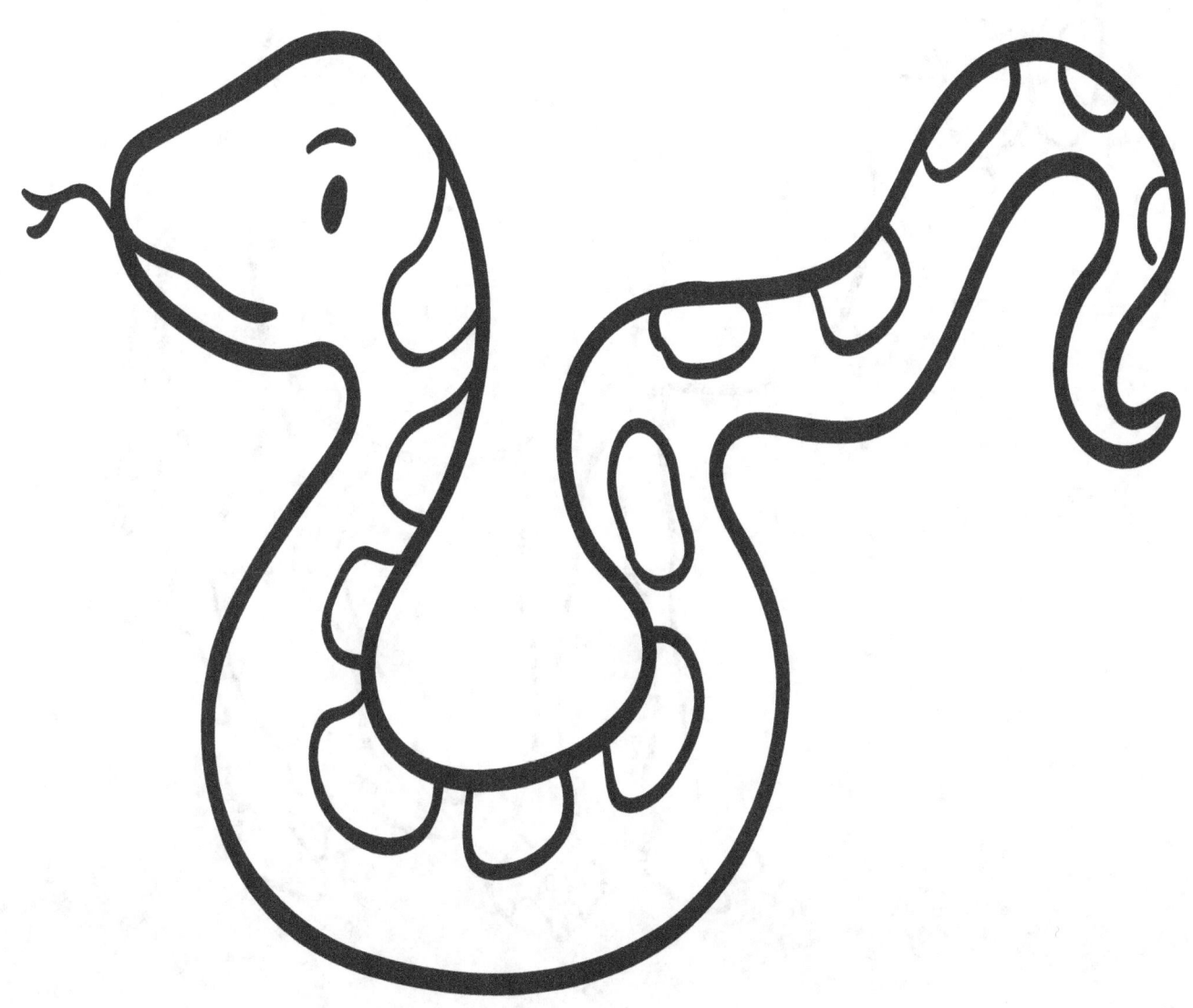

COLOR ME !

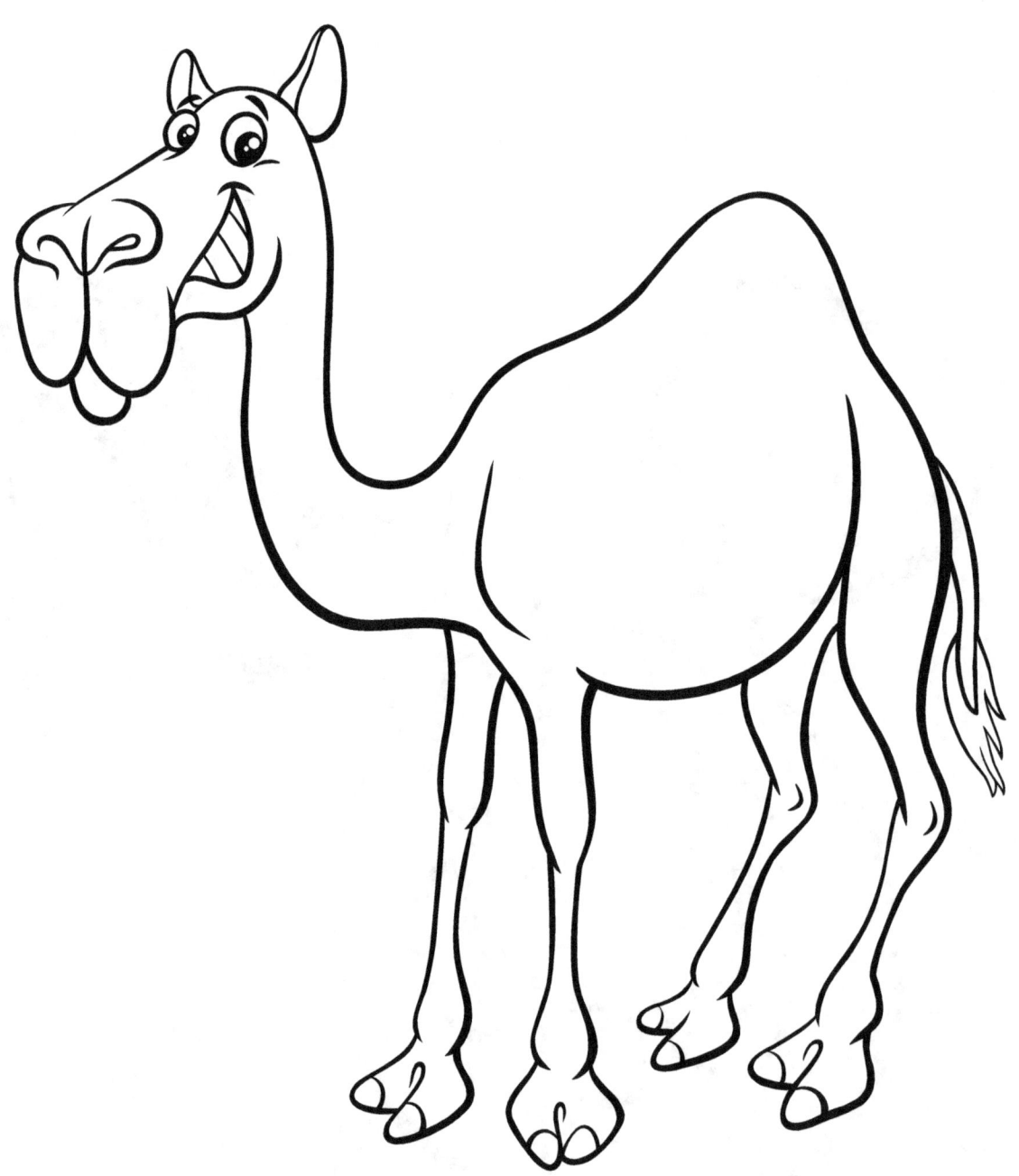

COLOR ME !

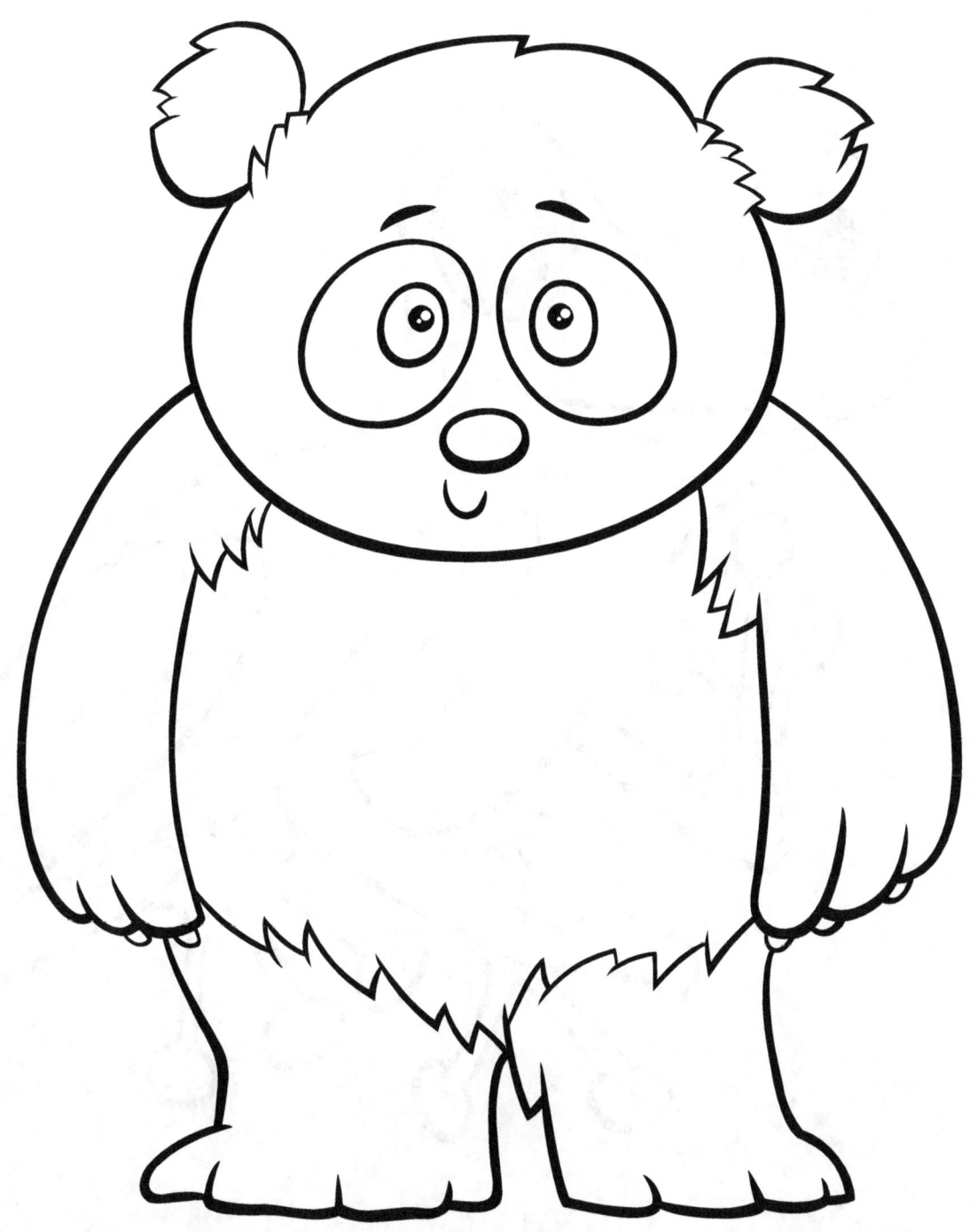

COLOR ME !

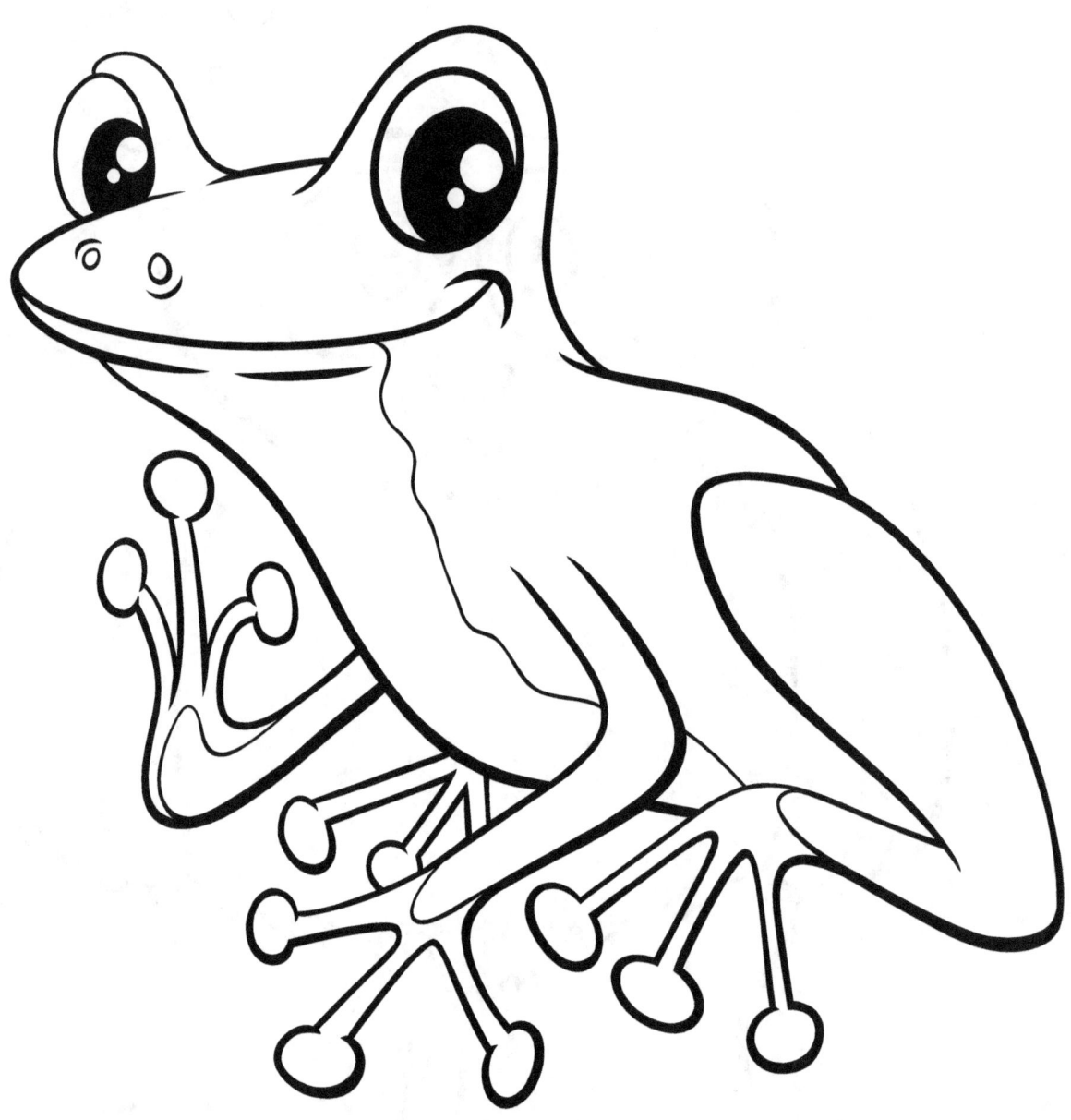

COLOR ME !

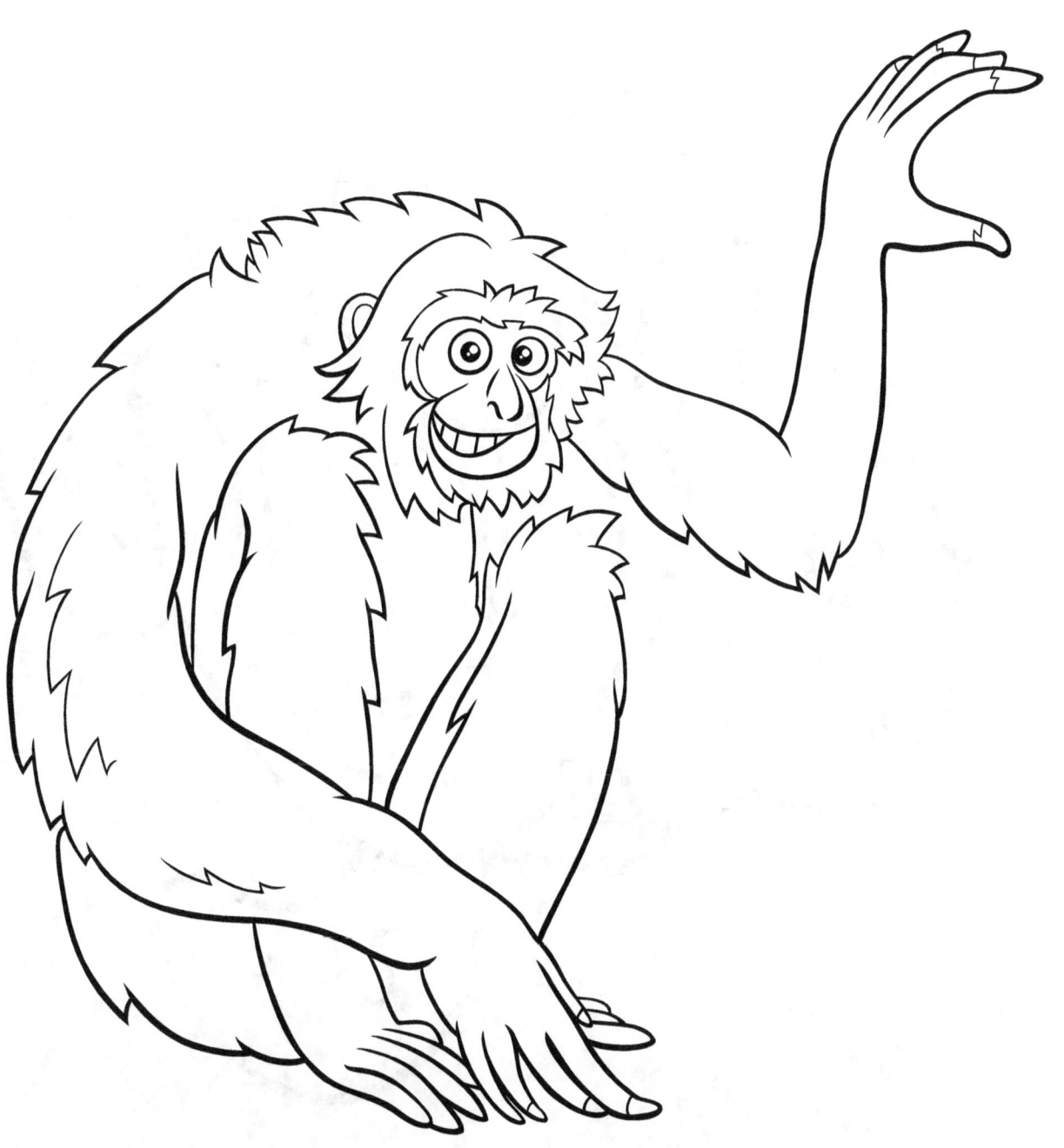

COLOR ME !

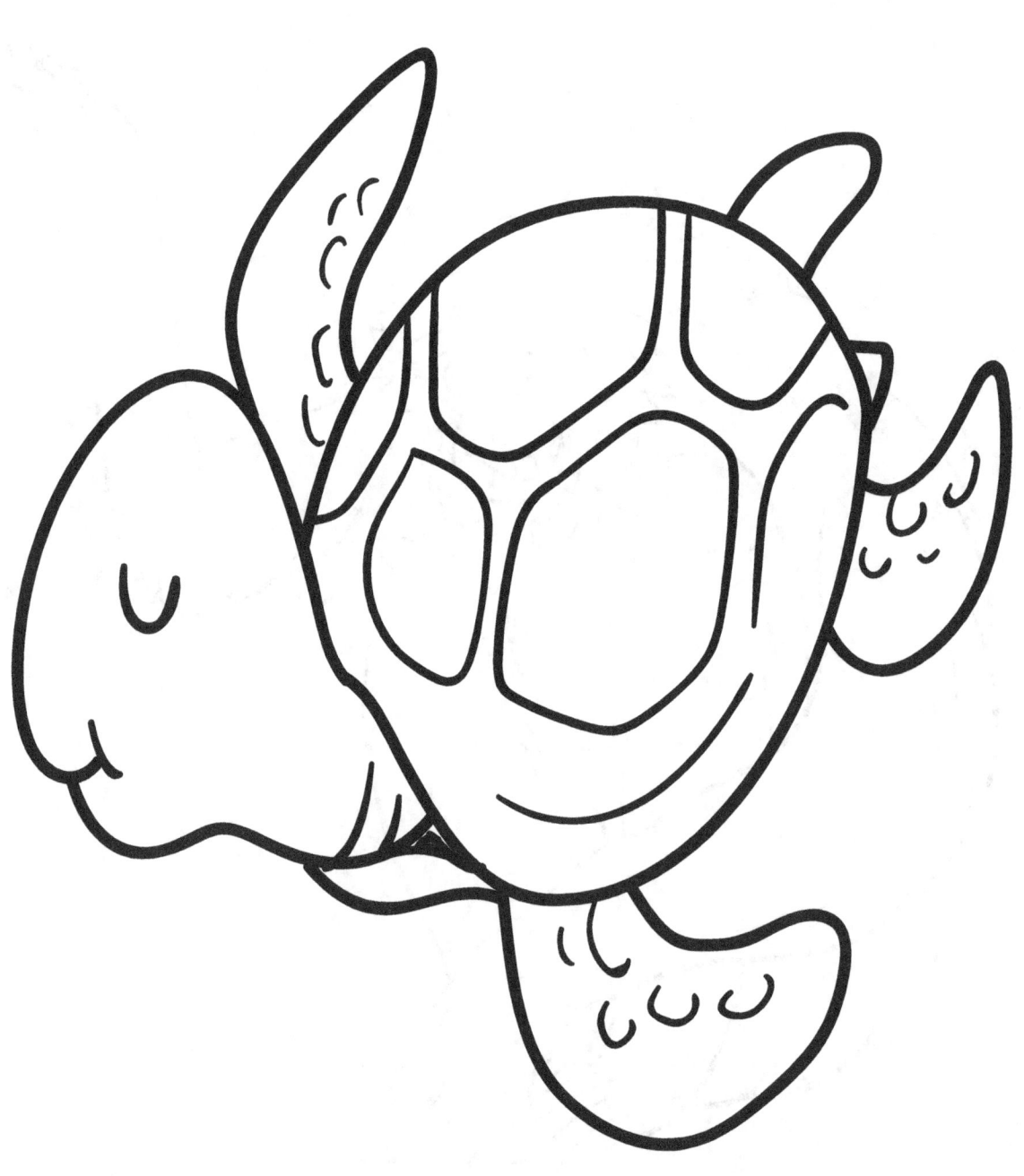

COLOR ME !

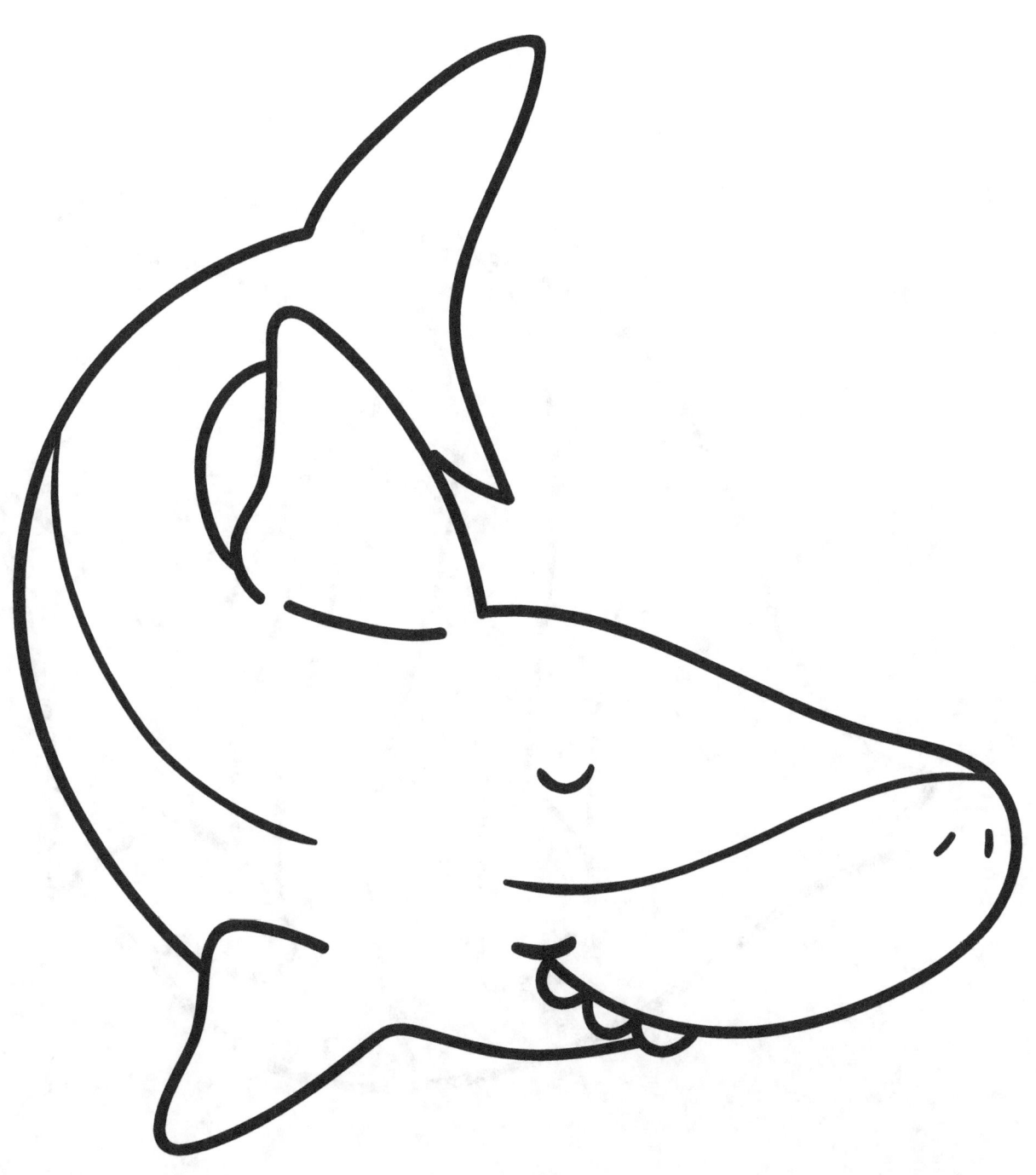

COLOR ME !

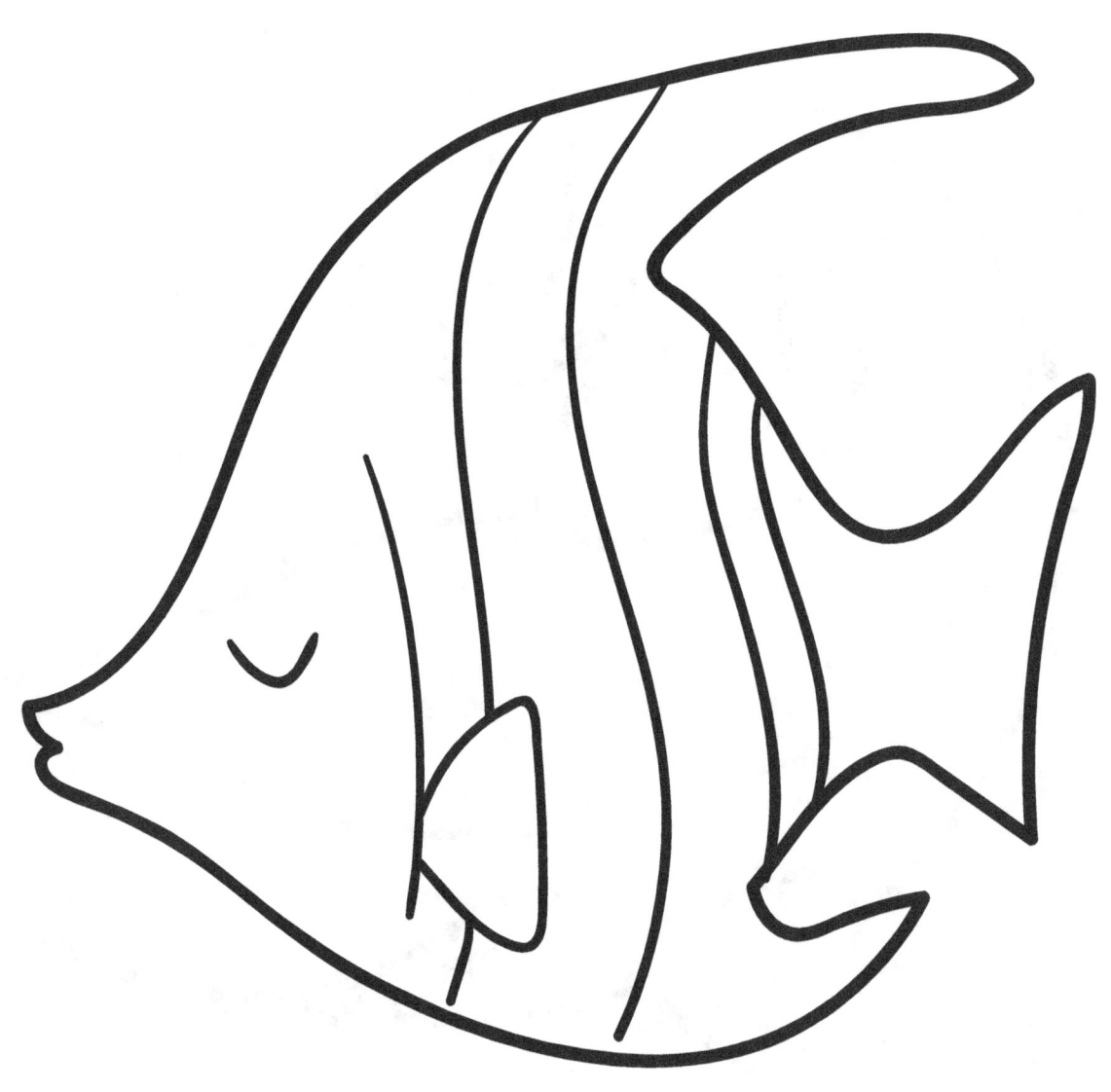

COLOR ME !

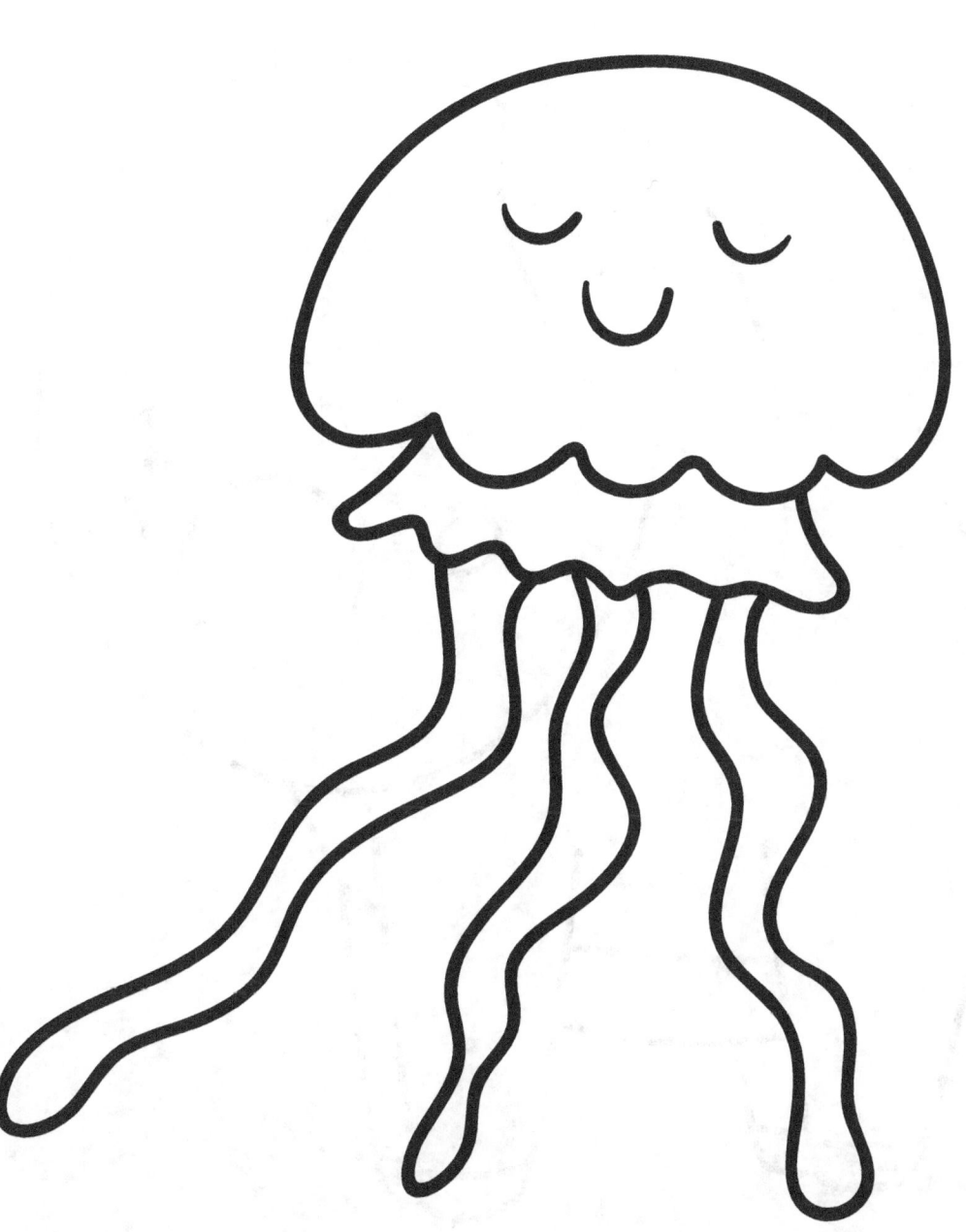

COLOR ME !

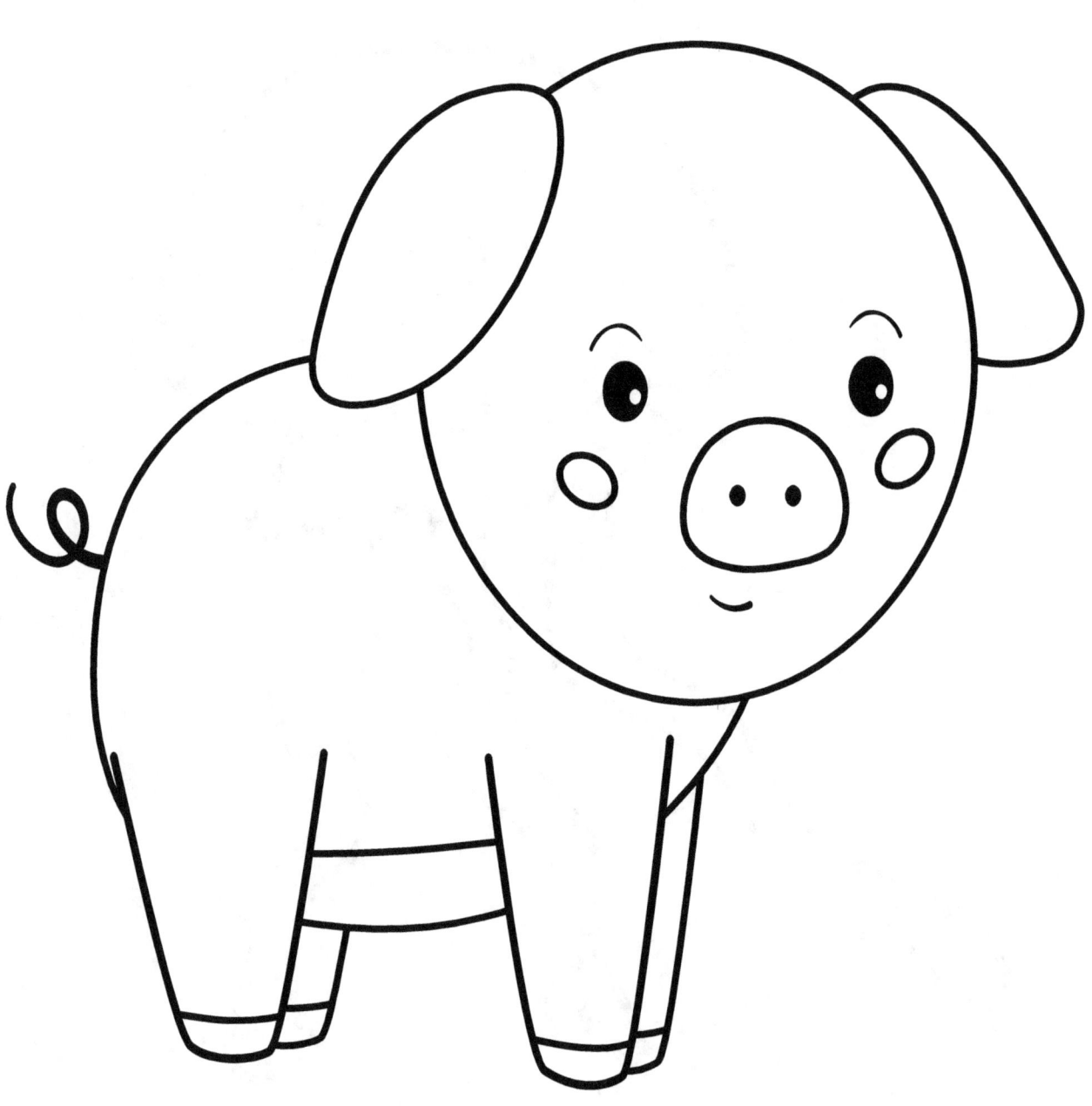

COLOR ME !

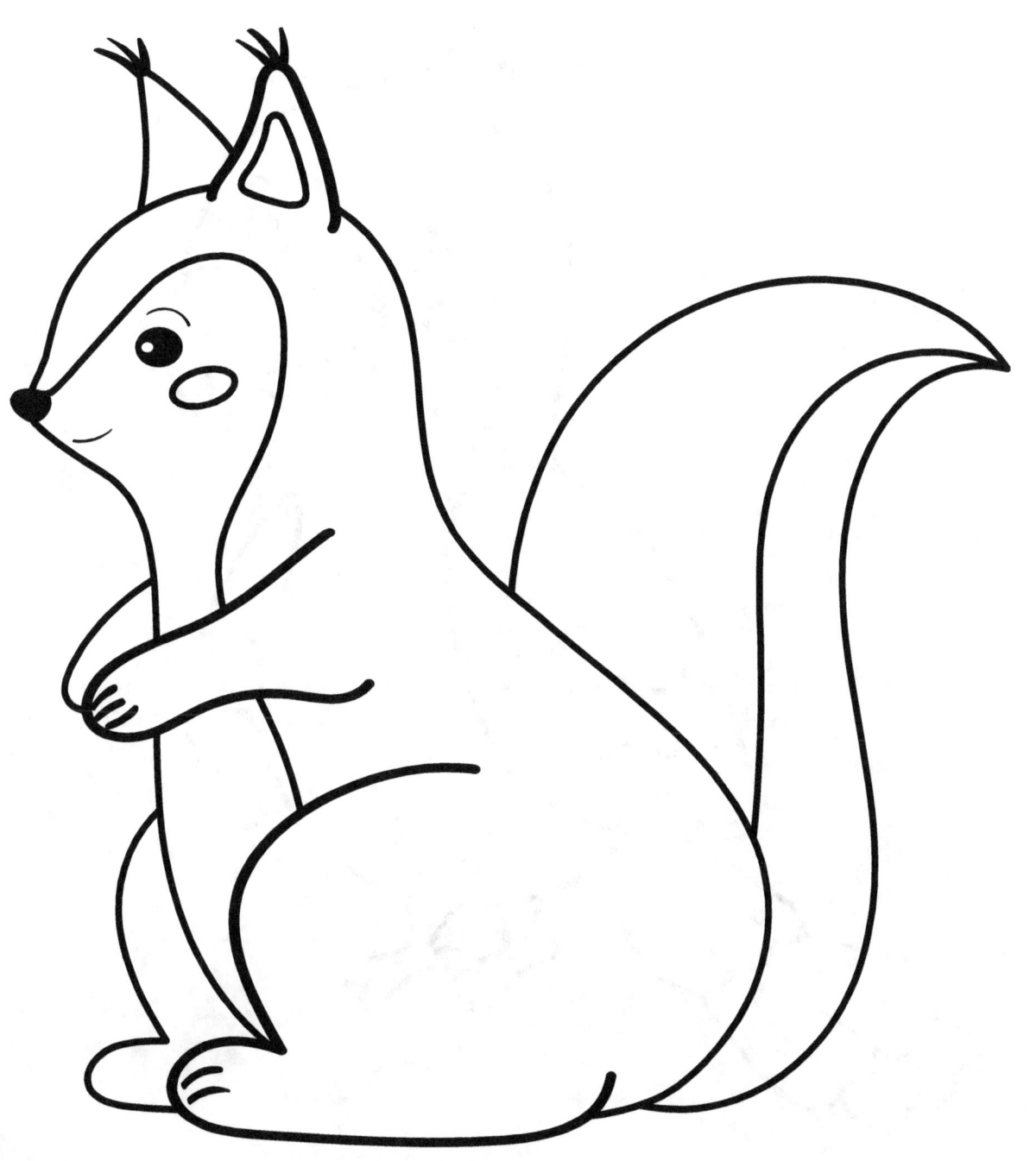

COLOR ME !

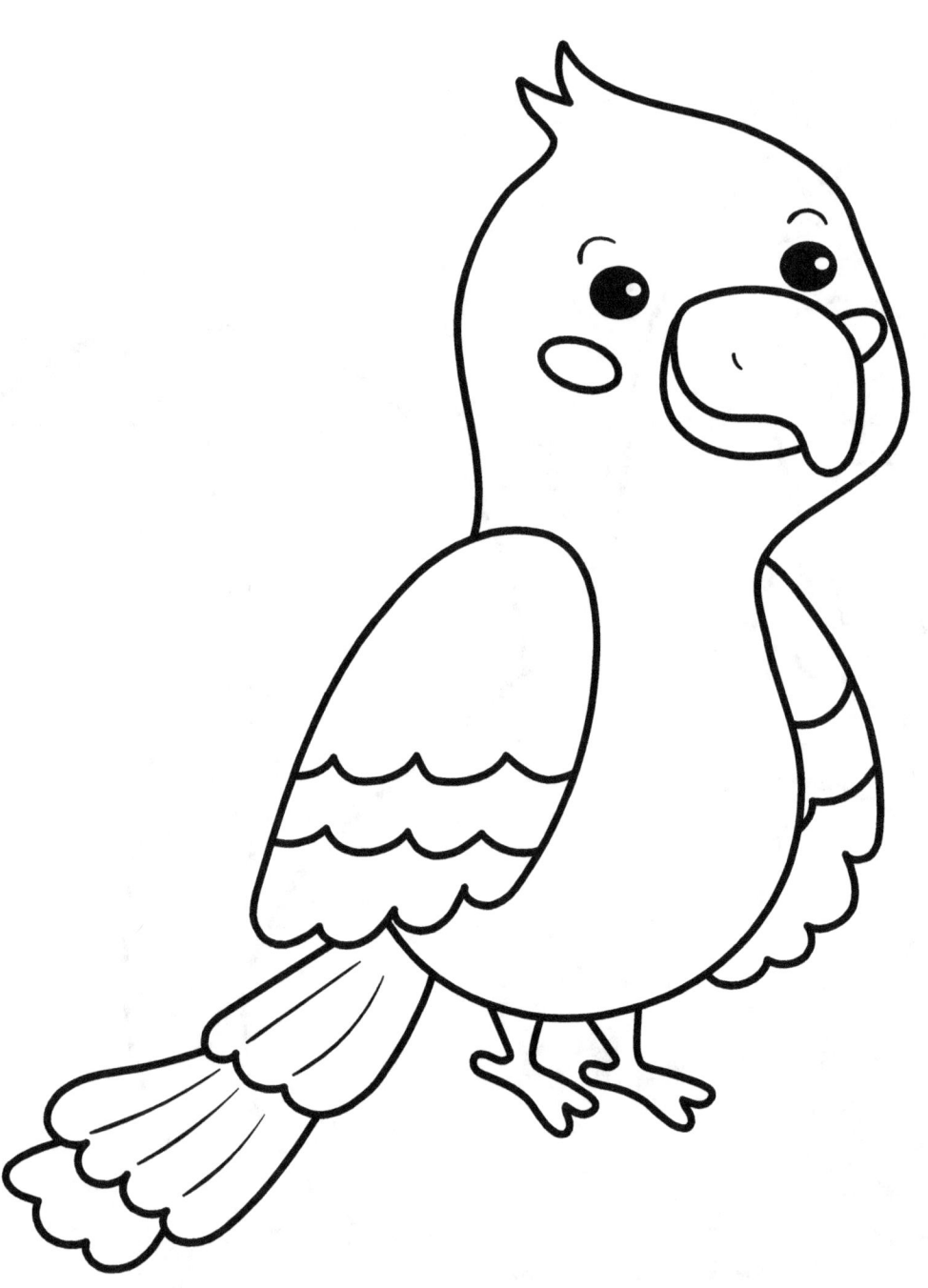

COLOR ME !

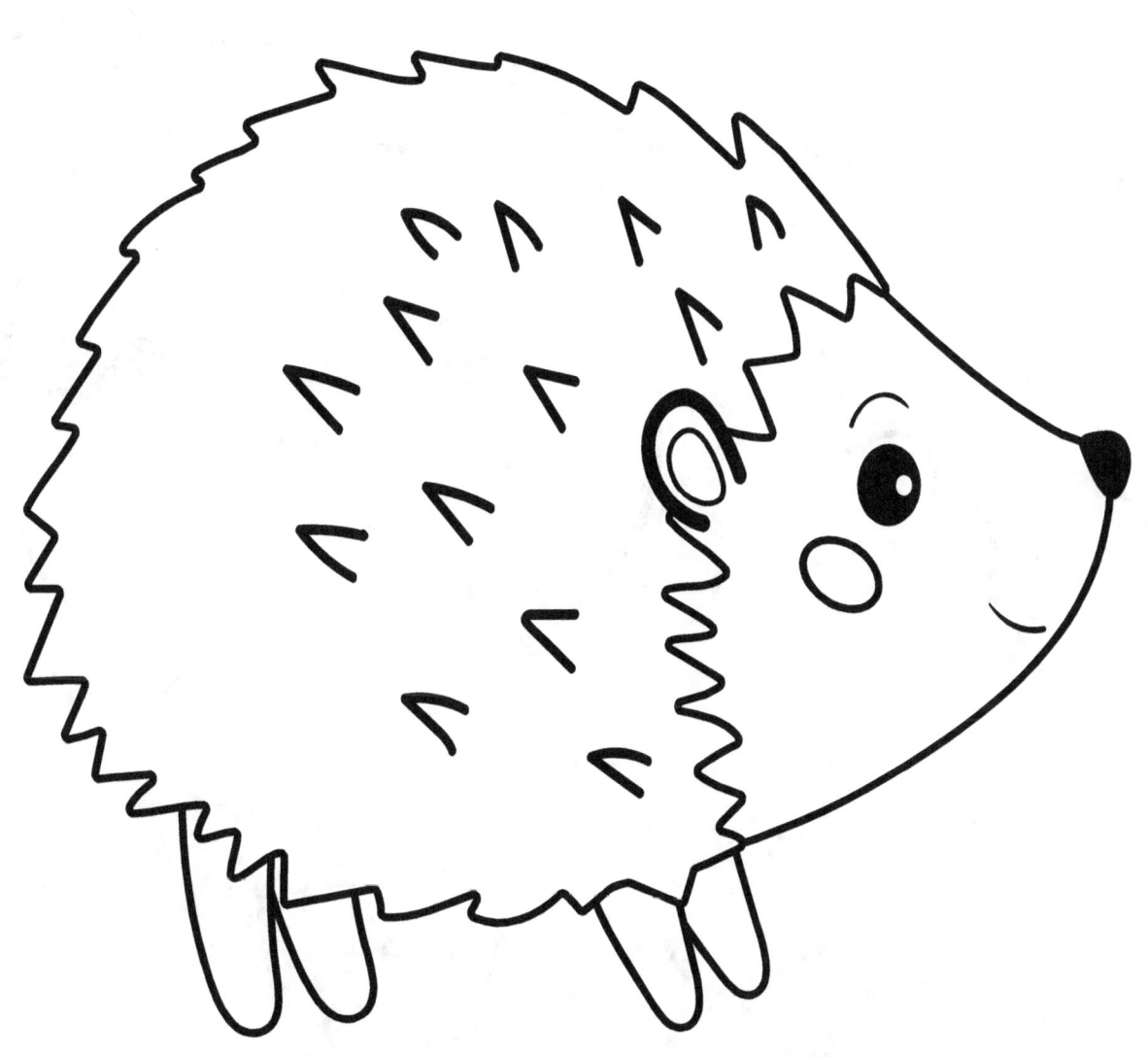

COLOR ME !

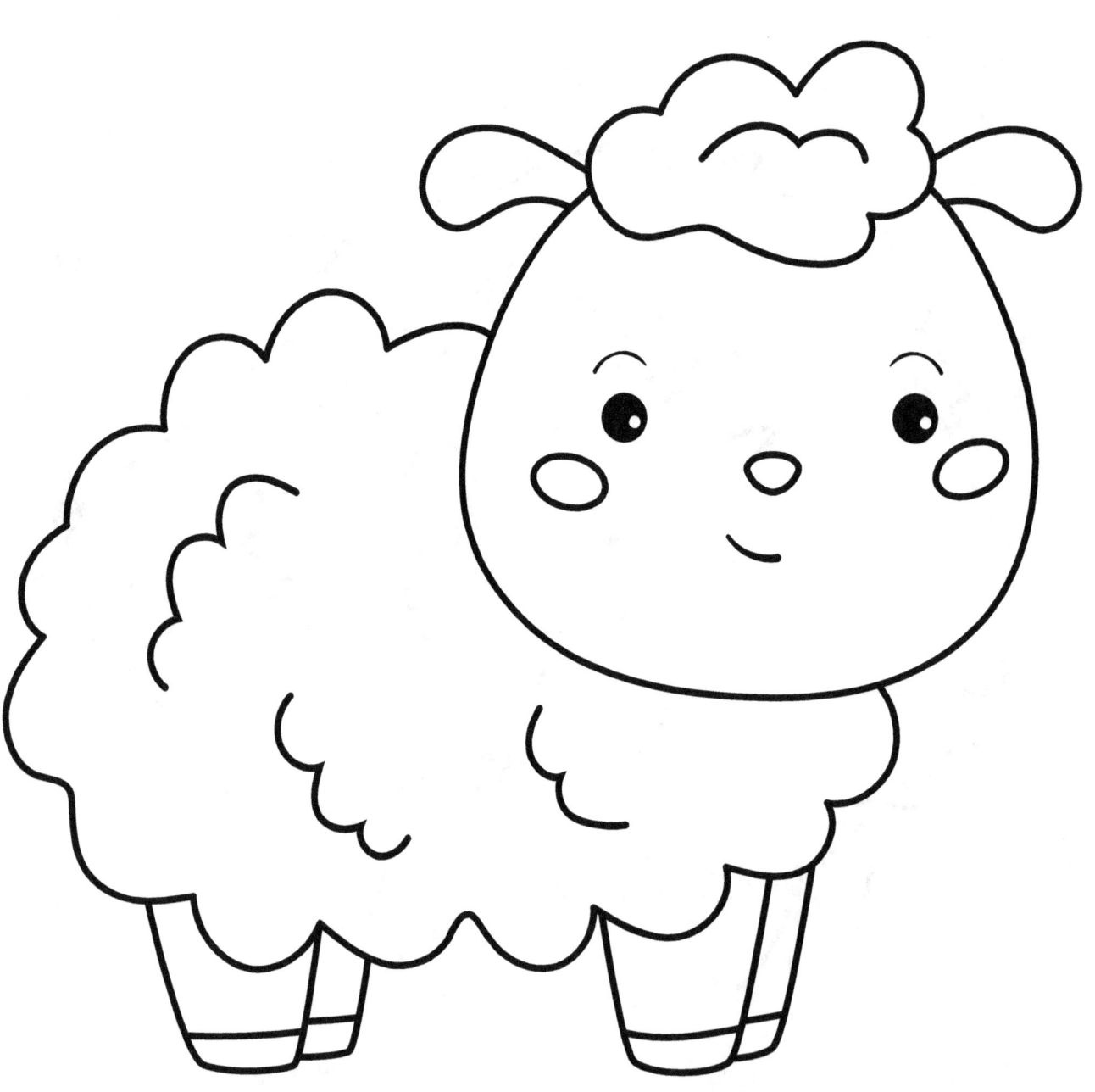

COLOR ME !

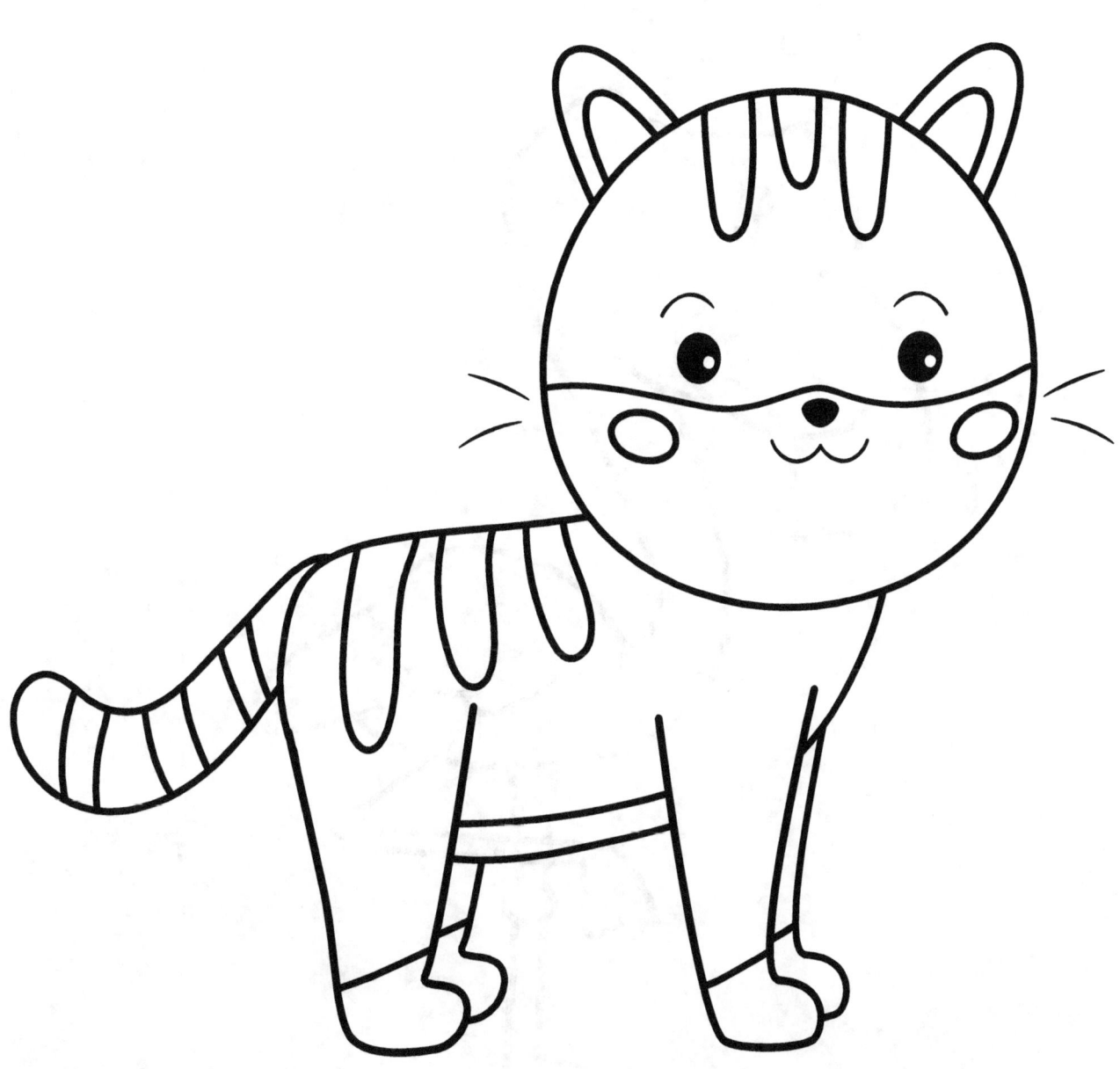

COLOR ME !

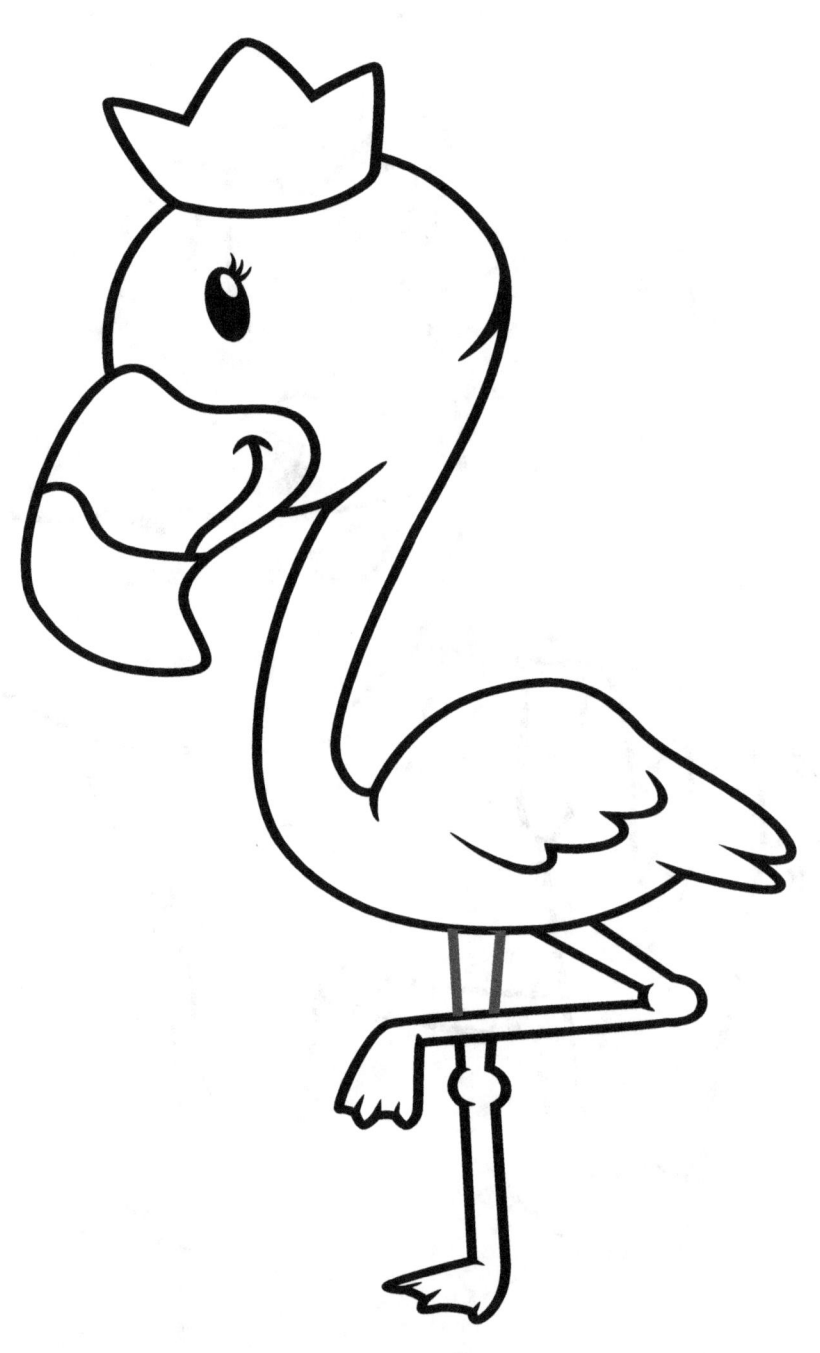

COLOR ME !

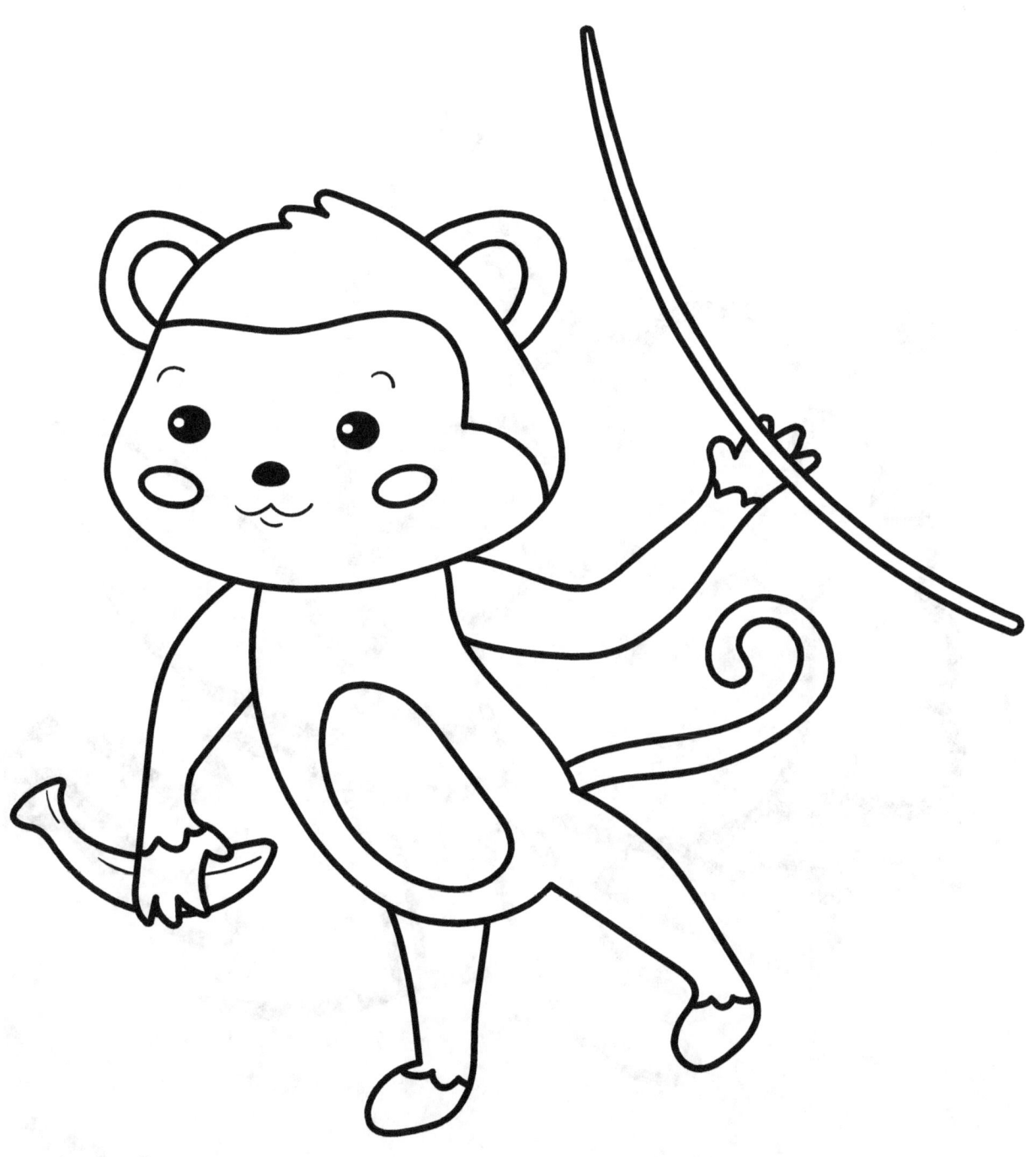

COLOR ME !

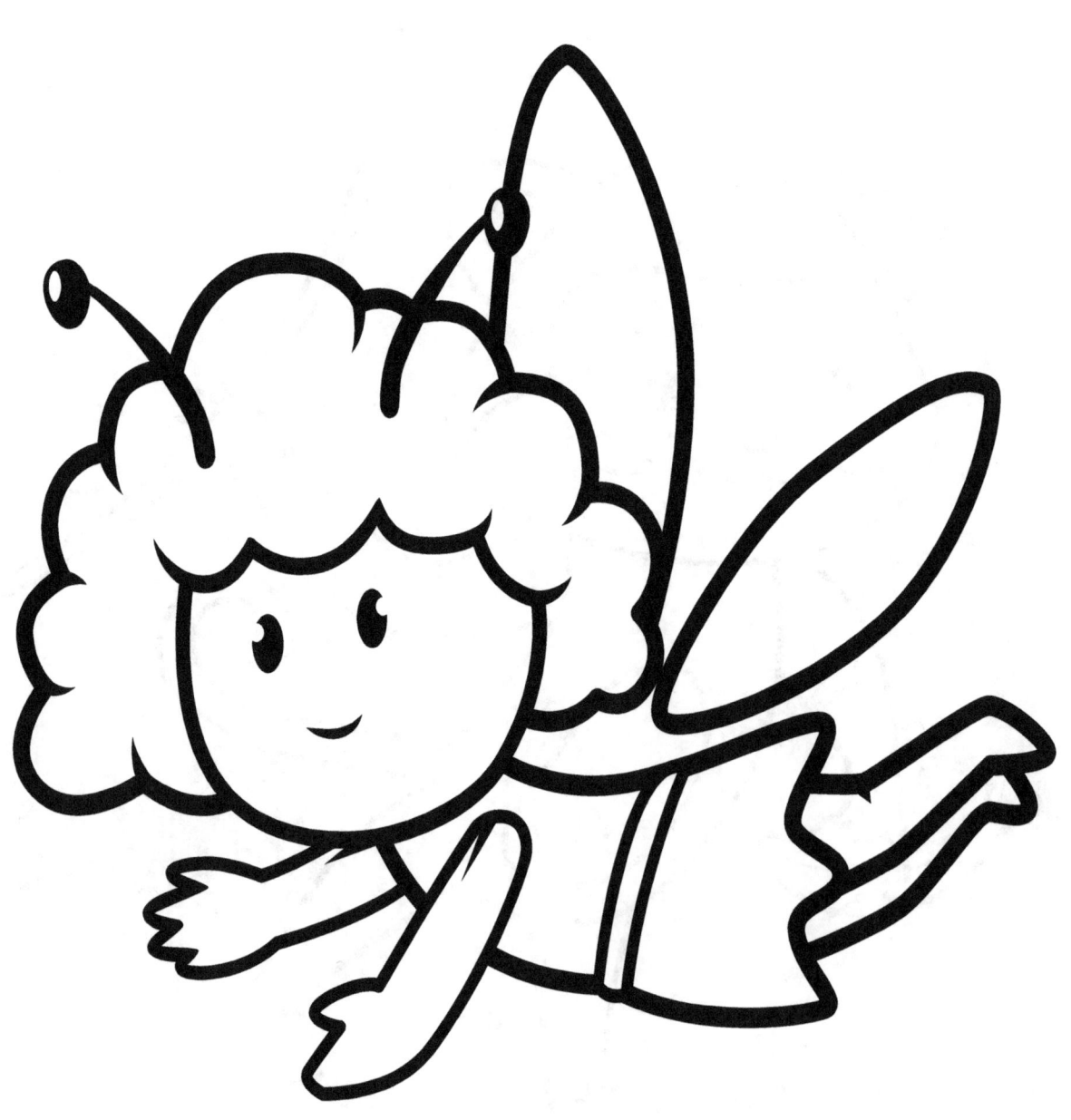

COLOR ME !

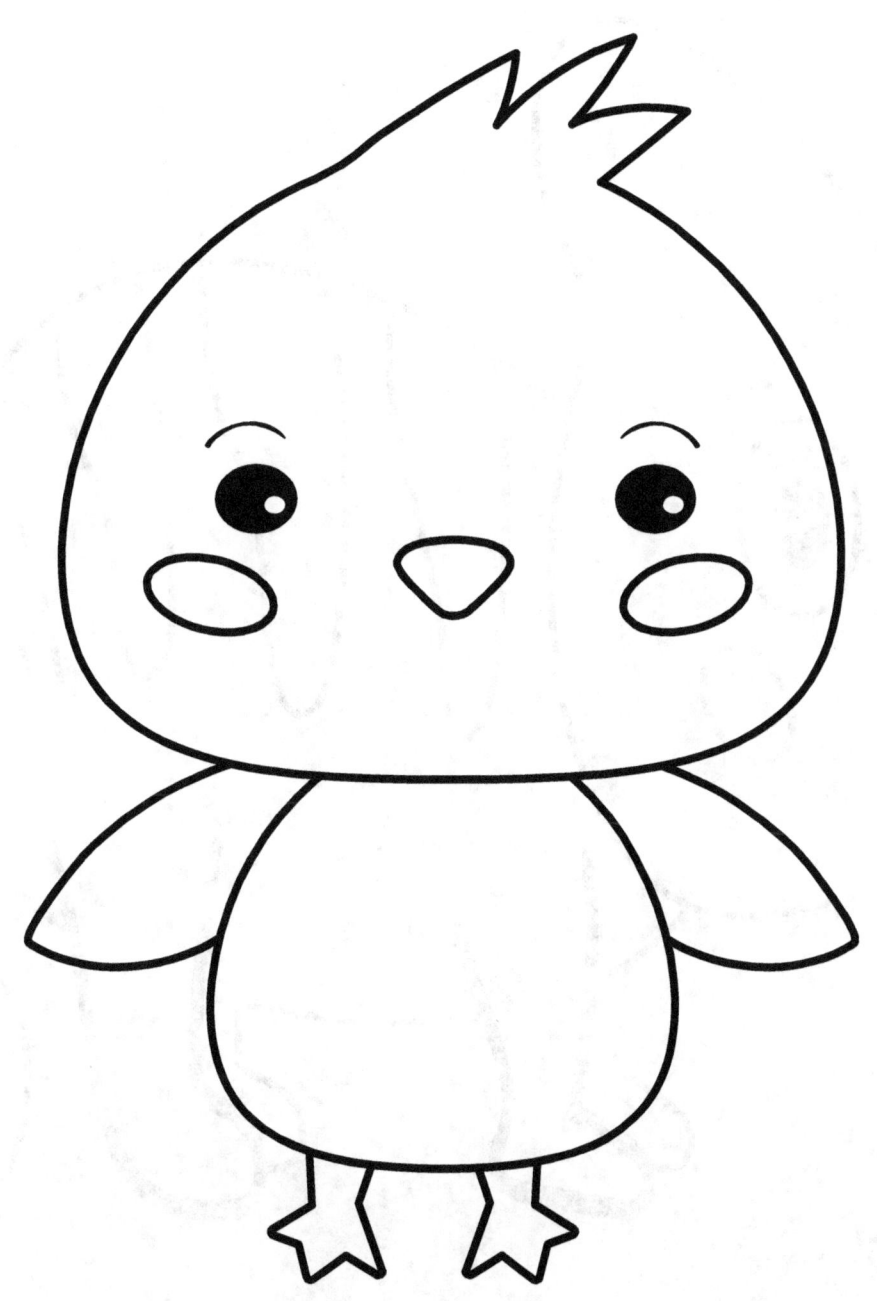

COLOR ME !

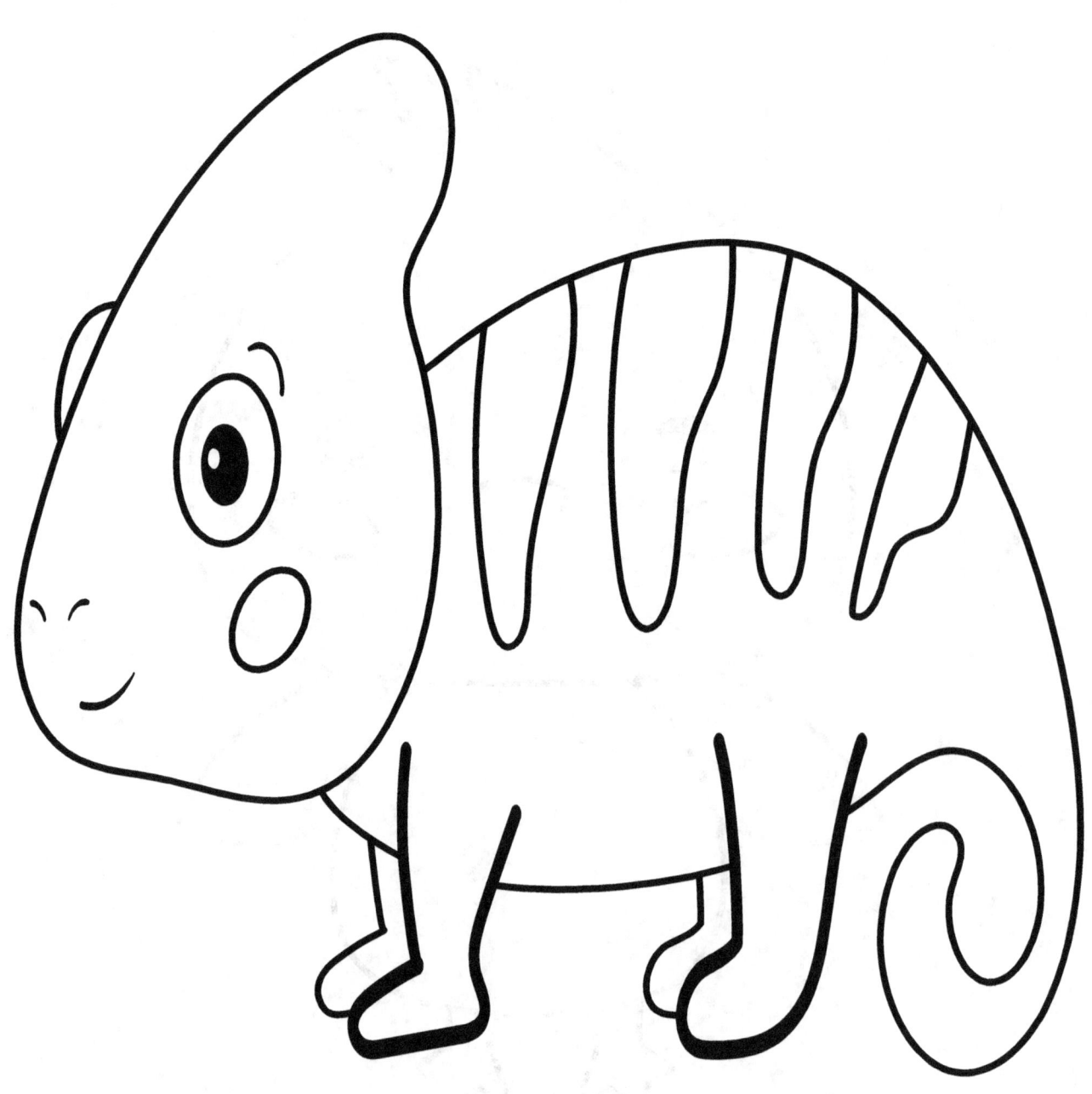

COLOR ME !

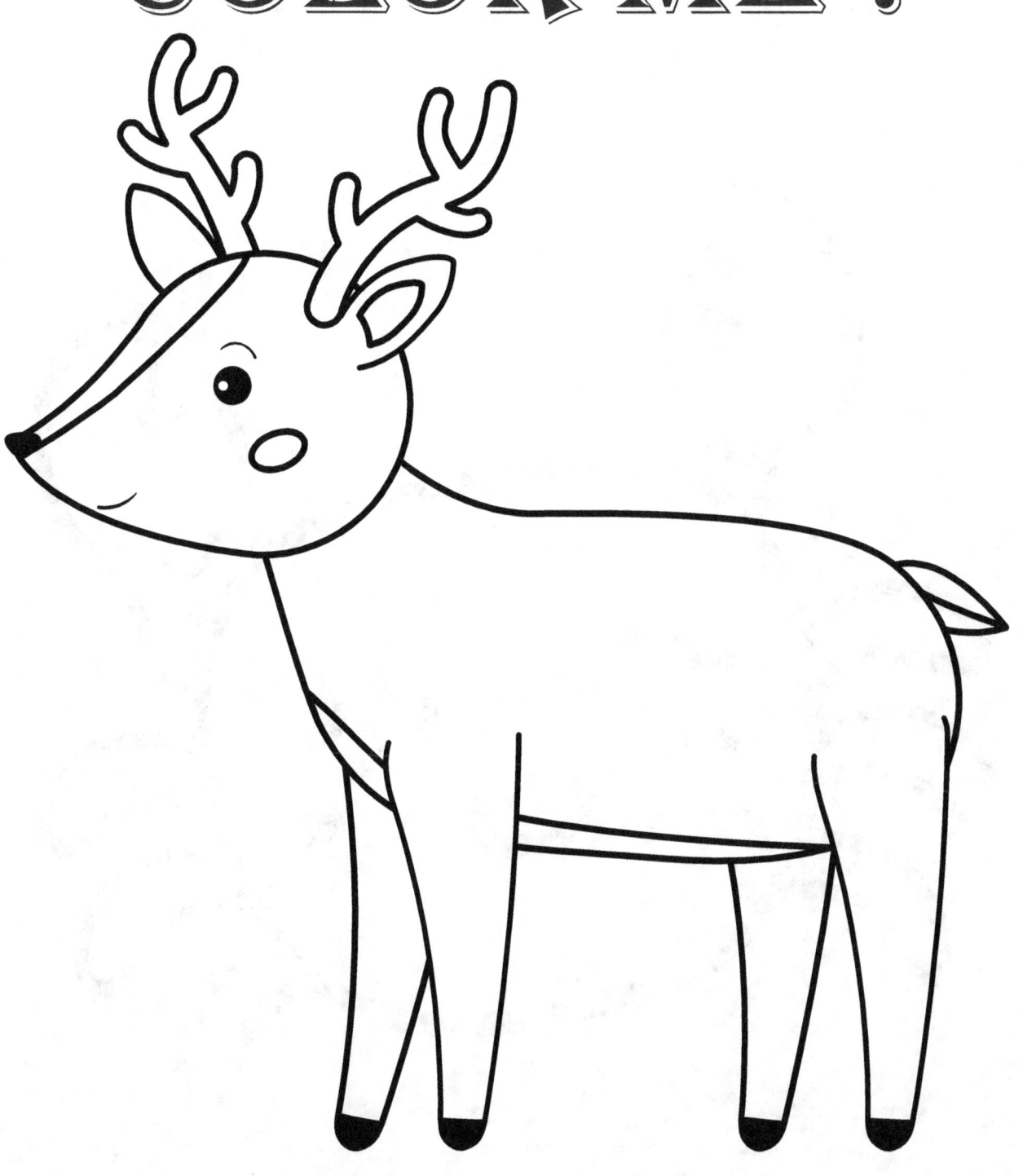

COLOR ME !

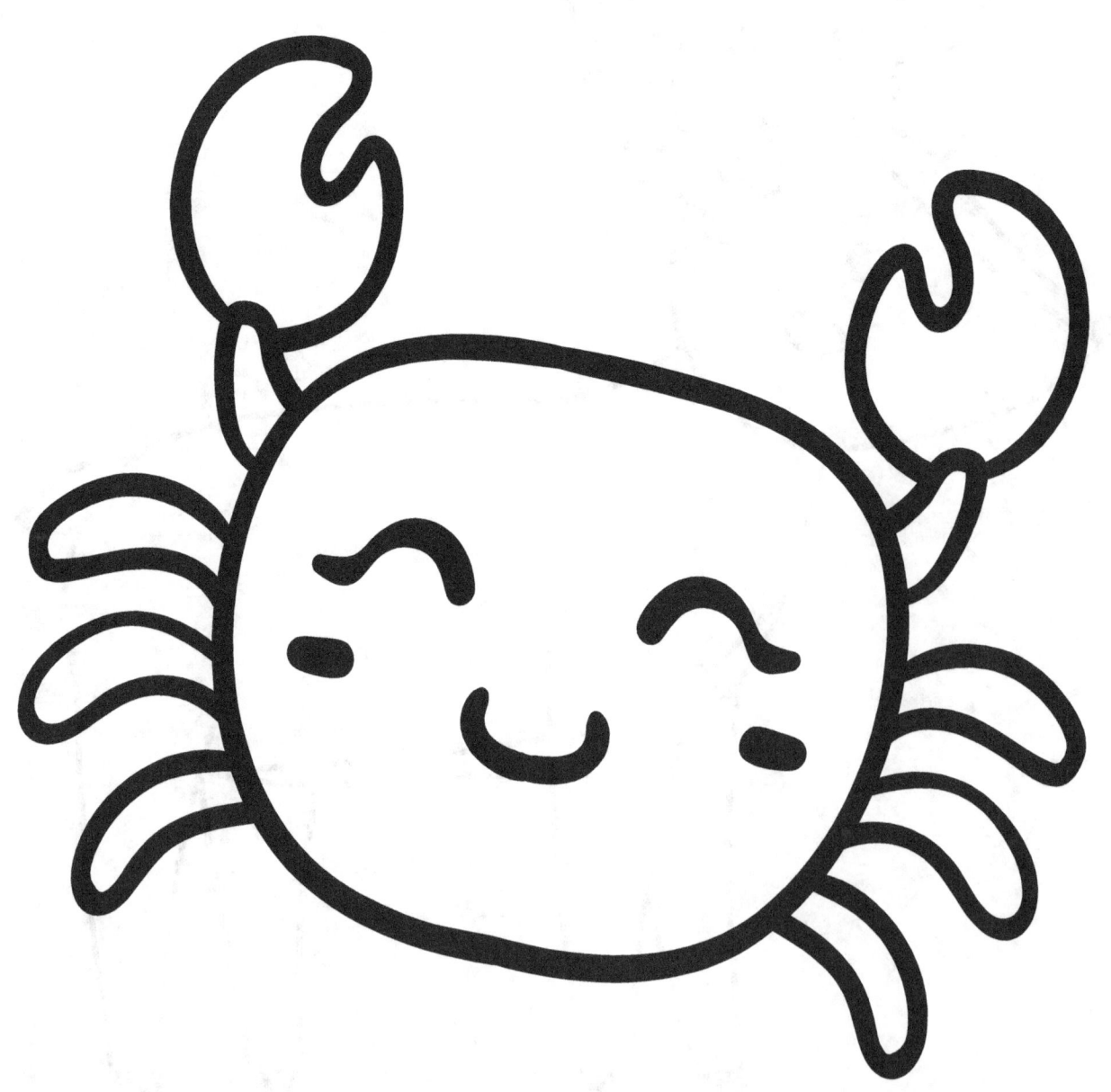

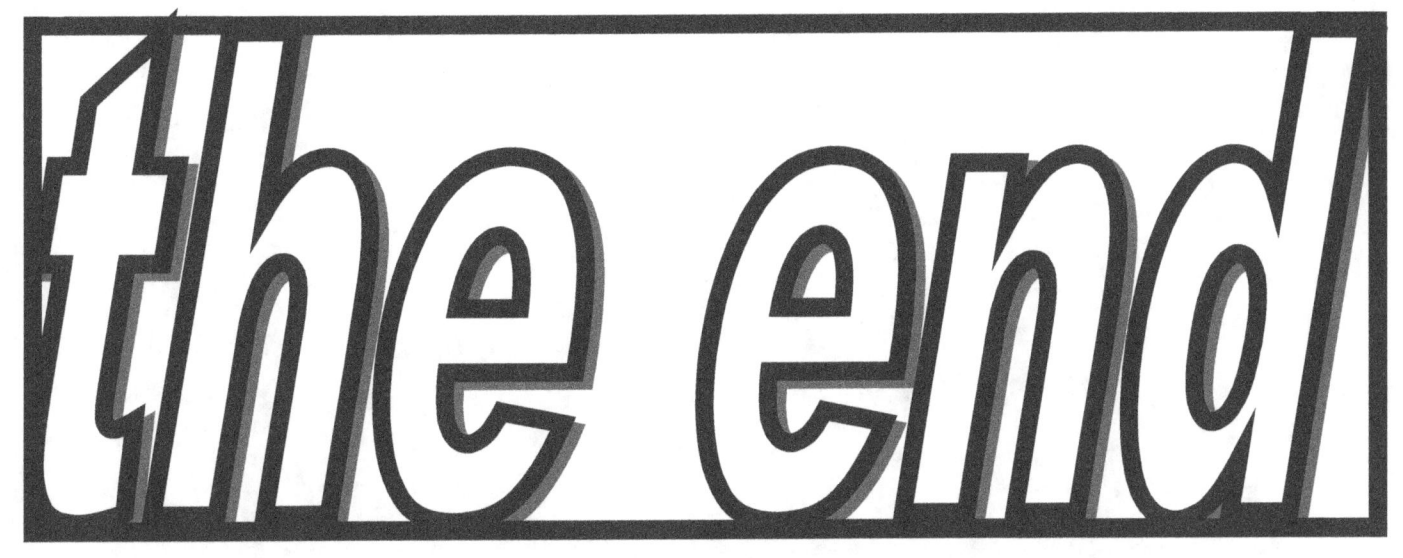

WE HOPE YOU

ENJOYED THIS COLORING BOOK